The Student Journalist
and
EFFECTIVE
WRITING STYLE

THE
STUDENT
JOURNALIST
GUIDE
SERIES

THE STUDENT JOURNALIST AND

EFFECTIVE WRITING STYLE

by
BRYAN REDDICK

PUBLISHED BY
Richards Rosen
Press, Inc.
New York

Published in 1976 by Richards Rosen Press, Inc.
29 East 21st Street, New York, N.Y. 10010

Copyright 1976 by Bryan Reddick

First Edition

Library of Congress Cataloging in Publication Data

Reddick, Bryan.
    The student journalist and effective writing style.

    (The Student journalist guide series)
    SUMMARY: Guidelines for improving one's ability to write in such a way as to efficiently and effectively communicate information.
    1. English language—Rhetoric. [1. English language—Rhetoric. 2. Communication] I. Title.
II. Title: Effective writing style.
PE1408.R39   808'.042   75-44487
ISBN 0-8239-0352-4

Manufactured in the United States of America

ABOUT THE AUTHOR

BRYAN REDDICK is Chairman of the English Department at Olivet College in Michigan. In his twelve-year career as college teacher, Dr. Reddick has offered courses in writing, language, and literature at several other colleges as well, including Syracuse, the University of California at Davis, The American University in Washington, D.C., and the universities of Lyon, Nice, and Grenoble in France. Before devoting his energies fulltime to graduate study of literature and to college teaching, Dr. Reddick worked as a  bellhop, an actor and comedian, and a printer's apprentice. He has been a newspaper reporter in Texas and Iowa, and for three years was a sportscaster and radio announcer in Iowa City.

Son of the prominent journalism educator Dr. DeWitt C. Reddick of the University of Texas, who wrote the well-known textbook *Journalism and the School Paper*, Bryan Reddick studied journalism in junior and senior high, where he was editor of the All-American school paper *The Austin High Maroon,* and at the University of Iowa, where he was graduated with honors, Phi Beta Kappa, in 1964. He has received many educational honors including two highly regarded postgraduate awards, the N.D.E.A. Fellowship (1966–69) and the Fulbright Teaching Fellowship (1969–70). He received a Ph.D. in English from the University of California at Davis in 1969, at the age of 27.

Dr. Reddick has published several articles on modern literature in national quarterlies, including essays on Joyce, Proust, and Lawrence. He is currently working on a text about writing fiction.

5

CONTENTS

PREFACE

I wonder if some future dictionary will record accurately the way we use the word *grammar* in ordinary conversation today. It surely is not used, on the occasions I am thinking of, to mean "the system of inflections and syntactical usages characteristic of a language." Rather, we often use the word *grammar* to mean something broader and more concrete, something like "the principles of effective writing."

This book grew out of a lecture delivered at the University of Texas in March, 1975, at the annual Interscholastic League Press Conference (Dr. Max R. Haddick, Director) of high-school journalists and their teachers. The lecture was called "Grammar: Thumb Your Nose or Rules of Thumb?" But even as I wrote that title, I knew I was not really going to talk about *grammar,* precisely speaking; and this book is not, precisely speaking, about *grammar* either.

There is a certain logic, and even moral force, to the argument that leads to the teaching of transformational grammar in junior and senior high schools (as is the current practice in Texas). This "new grammar" is the most precise and most accurate means we have of describing how our language works, how it lives and adapts to ever-changing needs and circumstances, and how it shapes and conveys meaning. It would seem beneficial for every native speaker of that language to know, consciously, what are its essential features, as a means both of knowing himself and his culture and of helping to shape himself and his culture.

On the other hand, it has been my consistent experience that any *abstraction* about language, even the truest of abstractions, is more likely to hinder a young person from learning to write effectively than to help. This was true when I myself was going through school, being exhorted to memorize 25 "rules" governing the use of the comma; and it is true today when my niece is

9

being taught to draw byzantine and exotic diagrams symbolizing the syntactic structures we do, in fact, use for communication.

We learn to write best by actually doing it, replacing all conscious, abstract concepts with intuitive and concrete habits. The purpose of this book is to contribute to the forming of useful habits, rather than to contribute to knowledge *per se*. The "grammatical terms" I have been unable to avoid using are the oldest, most pragmatic, most universally understood I know of. As much as possible they relate to concrete meaning and not merely to abstract "structures."

My aim is to provide no more than "just enough" to make it possible for a young writer to *look* at his or her writing, to notice where and in what respects that writing fails to communicate information effectively, and to feel she or he is capable of strengthening such weak spots. This seems worth doing, even though it may not contribute directly to a self-conscious, conceptual understanding of the language we are using. That task I am content to leave to others.

BRYAN REDDICK

INTRODUCTION

This book is organized in four general parts. To many it may seem that the real core of the text is to be found in Part 2, **Correctness,** in which more of the usual kind of general recommendations about such matters as punctuation, syntax, and pronouns are offered than in any other section. Such recommendations, however, cannot have much value without another kind of study, that which is found in Part 3, **Effectiveness,** in which general guidelines for improving one's writing *style* are offered. What we usually call "correct grammar" is not enough by itself to insure effective communication. A conventional or standard verbal pattern does not communicate unless it is *meaningful*. Part 3 suggests how a student can consider the question of meaning right along with the traditional questions of standard usage.

Furthermore, no textbook can teach a person to write well. Only experience, particularly the experience of writing and then conferring about the written work with a sensitive reader (a teacher, an editor, a friend), can truly help a person improve his or her particular writing skills. General suggestions can be made, of course, by those of us who have had experience as writers, teachers, and editors. But every writer has to consider very carefully just which suggestions actually apply to his or her own personal writing habits, and even to each specific writing assignment she or he attacks. Concrete, particular experience in writing is the best teacher, far surpassing the value of abstract or general textbooks.

To help compensate for this built-in inadequacy of a book that is, after all, designed to help the student learn to improve his or her writing, Part 4, **Revision,** offers one extended example of how effective rewriting of the article or essay can best be accomplished. Obviously, such an example will not apply in all ways to any particular writing task you actually undertake yourself. But the painstaking, hard-nosed attention to detail demonstrated there should serve as an elaborate model of what every writer, alone or in collaboration with an editor or teacher, should do as he or she revises "the first draft."

Finally, recommendations about how to write effectively can be useful only if they are adapted as much as humanly possible to specific social and individual needs. Learning to write effectively today seems harder than it has seemed before. There are reasons for this, which it is wise to know, in a general way, before we set out to accomplish our main goal, improving our writing style. Part 1, **A Few Basic Principles,** describes what I believe to be the essential problems facing the young writer today and the best general method for resolving them.

A Few Basic Principles

Chapter I

THE PROBLEMS OF EFFECTIVE COMMUNICATION TODAY

Since the late 1960's, students and teachers have been hearing a rapid crescendo of uneasiness, concern, and finally outrage arising from all over the United States.

"Young people today," the cry has gone up, "don't know how to write!"

College English teachers, who only a few years earlier had felt so confident of their students' ability to communicate effectively in both speech and writing that the traditional courses in "freshman composition" were made optional in many universities, have now quite suddenly come to believe that the writing skills of most young people finishing high school today are far less adequate than they have ever been. At one university in the East, and perhaps at others, teachers and administrators are beginning to wonder if the old-fashioned year-long courses once universally required of young people entering college are now enough by themselves to help students acquire the skills necessary to communicate clearly and efficiently. Perhaps, they fear, even more work on basic writing skills is needed.

It has been particularly shocking to high-school and college teachers to discover that student journalists, those young people most obviously committed to the effective and rapid communication of information, appear today to have more trouble than ever before with what seem the most elementary principles of "good writing": grammar, punctuation, sentence structure, pronoun usage, effective writing style.

SEPARATING EMOTIONS FROM PRACTICAL NEEDS

Quite naturally, students themselves might feel offended by the charge that they "don't know how to write." It might seem that the puzzlement, the bitterness that teachers, parents, businessmen, and employers generally are expressing about the apparent lack of "basic skills" among young people today is merely part of the heralded Generation Gap, that yawning chasm supposedly separating the Old Fogies from the New World. From the other side as well, this seems a tempting assumption: we might imagine some old reactionary explaining what he sees as the inability of young people these days to control their pronoun references or to place the apostrophe correctly as the result of the Decline of the West, the abandonment of All Standards of Propriety, the slide of Civilization toward Barbarity!

Both views parodied here are, of course, crude and exaggerated. The temptation to place the need for adequate communication skills into this essentially political context can only cloud the issue, obscuring the real problem with highly volatile emotional concerns that are in themselves real, human, and very significant, but are not truly relevant to the question of learning to write effectively.

As we shall see, there is genuine cause to establish a link between what is perceived to be the need for more rigorous training in informational writing and what is felt as a possible conflict of values. But the temptation to become emotional, either out of a desire to defend Youth in its fight against Authority, the rights of the Individual from a repressive Society, or on the other hand, from a conservative wish to maintain a highly valued Status Quo, should be resisted by us all. That will not help young people learn to write more effectively, and it will not help their teachers resolve what is obviously a serious, and a growing, problem.

KINDS OF COMMUNICATION

It is natural to associate the practical need for better writing skills with these emotional and moral concerns for at least two reasons. For one thing, language is intimately related to thought, and so the attempt to influence a person's writing habits is, in a sense, a direct attempt to influence the way he thinks.

This point is often made as one positive reason for improving one's writing style: improve your writing, improve your thinking! On the other hand, of course, a person might resent having his or her thinking meddled with in the first place.

I was myself arguing this case, taking the traditional line, with a rather aggressive young man back in the 1960's when activism and confrontation were in fashion. The conversation was not going well, the student deeply resenting my efforts to teach him to write more effectively, and I on my side not even able to sense exactly what he was trying to say.

Finally I understood. He was, in effect, making the following claim: "I have a right," he was saying, "to think *vague thoughts!*"

Now, that is true; I had to admit it, once I understood his position. On the other hand, I was not convinced that I should stop trying to help my students see the usefulness of clear, precise expression. (Clarity and precision would have been helpful during that very discussion, as a matter of fact.)

Such resentment is not silly or insignificant. It can be created by claiming too high a value for efficient, communicative prose. The simple conveying of information, what we teachers often call "expository writing" and what journalists are professionally concerned with all the time, is not the only kind of communication necessary among human beings, not even the only kind that employs language. In fact, such simple communication may not be, for you or for me personally, the most deeply important use of language. As a student and teacher of literature much of my time, I could hardly claim it was.

Some things in life, and among them those things most valuable, most profound, could not be called "information" at all; and simple, straightforward communication of them in ordinary, everyday words and sentences just is not possible. In our interpersonal relationships we use gestures, facial expressions, tone of voice, touching, and so on, to communicate our deepest and most important meanings. On other occasions we might use music, dance, painting, or sculpture to "communicate" this sort of thing. In the verbal realm, of course, we use poetic, dramatic, or narrative *art*—which is a very different business from the simple communication of information.

For the individual, then, as a person alone and in direct relation with other persons close to him or her, simply conveying information may not be the most profoundly significant form of communication.

SOCIETY AND INFORMATION

Still, the efficient communication of information probably is the most important use of language from a more broadly *social* point of view.

At least since the Renaissance it has seemed important to people in the Western world to consider themselves not only in relation to those in their immediate family and in the town where they lived, but also in relation to thousands—even millions—of other people, possibly living in other countries or at other times in history, whom they would never even see, let alone know as individual persons. To make possible this broad notion of the self in relation to so many others, a highly uniform type of language was evolved in every Western nation that would be comprehensible even to those who had no knowledge of the person speaking or, more often, writing it.

Today, of course, we take such interchange across time and space for granted. Most of us do not even notice, for example, how often and how easily we are able to communicate every day of our lives with people whom we do not know personally at all. What seems to us the natural business of ordinary living depends on this essential ability. Consider, for example, how many times in a single day you yourself communicate to others whom you do not know personally, and they to you. The stranger who stops you in the hall to ask directions to the Principal's office. The clerk in the drugstore who sells you a candy bar or a roll of film. The telephone operator who tells you the new number of that friend of yours in physics class. The admissions officer of that private school in Florida you have heard about, whom you ask in a letter to send a catalog. And so on and so forth ad infinitum.

Even in a small town, communication among strangers is today an integral feature of everyday life. At the very least, people living in a small town read newspapers, books, and magazines written by persons they do not know, who in turn do not know them either. We might even say that much of what we see and hear on radio and television has this feature as well: speaker and hearer do not know each other personally. Rather, in all these forms of communication, what seems to matter is not the person writing or speaking, and not the person she or he is addressing. What matters most is the impersonal subject about which he or she is talking or writing.

This kind of communication, then, which is so crucial to all our normal modes of social interaction, is essentially impersonal, we might say "matter-of-fact."

For social purposes and also for all broad social interaction from the individual's own point of view, the ability to exchange information rapidly and precisely is so convenient, so eminently useful, that to most of us today it seems vitally necessary. Still, we might cause unnecessary confusion and stir up needless resentment if we did not recognize that the impersonal communication of information, which is the topic of this book and which is essential to our society, is not the only kind of communication, not the only use of language vital to our lives as individual, fully human persons.

PERSONAL AND PUBLIC LANGUAGE

We might contrast the language an individual uses as a whole person, a living self interacting with other selves immediately nearby, with the language that person uses in a broad social context among people he or she does not know well.

Such a "personal language" might be used for the individual himself, serving an inner need, to help get his thinking straight or to assert himself; or it might more often be used in an intimate interpersonal relationship, with parents, for instance, with friends, or very close associates. "Personal language" of this sort would not often be written. It would most often be *spoken,* in a certain tone of voice, accompanied by facial expressions, gestures, and so on. It would always be informed by a specific interpersonal context. Whether designed in a particular instance primarily to express emotion or not, it would always have a significant emotional content or meaning.

The "public language," on the other hand, with which the journalist or the essayist is concerned and which any person uses every day in his or her purely social activities, can be thought of as primarily *written.* It usually seems a neutral conveying of "facts" whose audience is not precisely known, being in fact that abstraction The General Public. "Public language," designed simply to transmit information, does not directly express its user's emotions, nor does it work directly upon its audience's emotions. I often say that this type of language does not "EX-press" nor does it "IM-press"; it merely communicates.

This second type of language does not embody in its form the personality either of the speaker or writer or of the listener or reader. Rather, "public language" conforms to *purely social norms.*

Learning to write this way, therefore, may indeed seem repressive. Writing strictly to communicate information does value social, public conventions over personal or individual feelings and characteristics.

But, rather than resenting the kind of social discipline exerted upon us to learn to communicate effectively this way, let us simply recognize the obvious usefulness this kind of "public language" may have, *as well as the limits of its usefulness.* So long as we recall that, in our fully personal lives, we may communicate, we may even use language in absolutely any way it seems meaningful, valuable, or just "fun" to do so, then perhaps we can work together to perfect our ability to write efficiently and anonymously without feeling overly oppressed or frustrated. Let us try, in any case, to keep these complex emotional issues from obscuring the simple, pragmatic functions of communicative writing.

SPECIAL PROBLEMS FOR EFFECTIVE WRITING TODAY

The "public language" I am discussing (and using!) here, the words and sentences we employ in order to communicate simple facts clearly and efficiently, seems to be peculiarly well suited to writing or even printing. Informational writing, that is, seems to be a highly *visual* form of communication, relying on our ability to *see* written or printed symbols and to invest them with a rather limited sort of significance. Most basically, of course, these symbols make up the alphabet in which all Western languages are written. Something about the nature of utilitarian language designed primarily to communicate information efficiently makes it especially well suited to the printed page.

This should not be too surprising. Consider how much voices vary. You can even recognize an individual friend or acquaintance by the distinct sound of her or his particular voice. The same is true, though in a lesser degree, of handwriting. Though a person's spoken language is translated into a visual representation in handwriting, that person's own peculiar and distinct individual traits may be observed in the particular way he makes his letters when writing.

In typewriting and printing this is no longer true. All letters appear more or less the same, no matter whose words are being represented by the visual symbols. In this way, the individual characteristics of the person who thought the language in the first place are greatly de-emphasized. Likewise, the printed text may be read and understood equally well by anyone, in just about any time or place. The peculiar traits of the individual persons understanding the words and sentences are also de-emphasized by the print medium.

As a result, the language in print tends not to call attention to itself, to its own peculiarities, emotional qualities, and so on. Printed words and sentences seem instead to become a "transparent" device through which a purely public or impersonal content or meaning may be transmitted. Emphasis in printed language tends to be on *what* is said, rather than on *who* is saying or hearing it. Printed language, that is, tends to be that form of communication most likely to be primarily designed to communicate simple information rapidly and clearly. The printed form emphasizes the information itself rather than the particular words and phrases by which the information is conveyed.

CONTEMPORARY CULTURE

In our culture today, printed language is much less dominant than it was in the Western world fifty or a hundred years ago. The electronic media—television, radio, telephones, even computers—have taken over much of our daily lives, reducing the degree to which we center our activities around printed and written communication. I believe it is sometimes felt that young people in our day are noticeably less oriented toward writing and reading than were their parents and earlier generations, and more oriented toward music, radio and television, movies, and so on. But this is really true of our whole culture. The electronic technology has changed all of our lives dramatically, lessening the predominant hold printed language has had upon Western culture for the past three or four centuries.

It may well be true, therefore, that it is harder today to learn to write effectively than it has been for a long time. In a culture which, like ours, is not entirely dominated by printed and written uses of informational language, a special effort is required for all of us who want or need to learn to use language to communicate information as precisely and quickly as possible.

THE SOCIAL NEED FOR COMMUNICATION

Although it is true that the simple conveying of information through the printed word is not as central a part of our culture as it was of our forefathers', the usefulness of communication skills must still be quite obvious. Most of the ordinary business of our daily, practical lives is conducted by means of the "'public language" whose characteristics we have been exploring. Social interaction is marked today, more than ever, by interchange among people who do not know each other personally and who must rely on a common means of communication that does not depend upon their individual traits, but upon social conventions of "public language." In this respect (as usual) our culture is growing cumulatively rather than sequentially. In other words, we have not left printed language behind in favor of the more instantaneous electronic media. Rather, we have incorporated the print media into a larger, more complex system. Within that system, which is contemporary culture, the practical utility of informational writing is still very evident.

Just as it is true that the printed word is not now as central a part of our world as it once was, it is also true that at no time in Western history has so much been printed and so much read.

Finally, no one could deny that especially in contemporary culture, in which the disastrous consequences of international misunderstanding are unmistakably clear, there is a peculiarly intense social necessity for all of us to be able to communicate simple, practical information clearly and efficiently. The need for adequate communication skills, then, is still with us, even though many aspects of our surrounding culture do not make it easy for us to acquire them.

DIFFERENCES BETWEEN SPEAKING AND WRITING

How does writing differ from speech?

For years teachers of "expository writing" have felt it necessary to stress the profound qualities speaking and writing have in common rather than to emphasize precisely how they differ. The reason for this is easy to understand. The worst thing that could happen to young writers would be to feel that they are not themselves fully in control of what they write, to sense that instead of being a practical skill they can use every day of their lives, writing is a kind of obscure "game" they must learn to "play" in order to please their teachers in school. The unfortunate fact is that some aspects of teaching and learning in school may create this impression. Especially is it easy to think that grammar and punctuation are alien and useless disciplines belonging only to sterile, old-fashioned schoolteachers if writing is thought of as a system of abstract *rules* that you must learn to follow more or less rigorously or else receive failing grades. So long as "English" was taught in the schools as a system of 25 comma rules, or something similar, any student might feel that it was not for his own real needs that he should learn to improve his writing style, but merely to please some abstract authority figure, perhaps a teacher, perhaps that awful enemy, The Establishment.

No, the language you write is essentially the same as that which you speak, at least when you are conducting business with someone you do not know personally. Rather than give you the impression that writing is a foreign element, merely an exercise you work on to please your elders, it is right to remind you that communication through language is basically the same either in speech or in writing.

Still, let's face it: there are some basic and obvious differences between written and spoken language.

In a culture that is apparently moving away from its traditional orientation toward the written and printed word but in which such visual, verbal communication still has vital importance, it seems like a good idea to recognize the essential differences between speech and writing as the areas that are most likely to require extra work.

The least we can say is that writing is the visual representation of speech, which in itself is oral (spoken) and aural (heard).

In order to translate a spoken thought or sentence into a series of visual signs, we need the alphabet, of course. Beyond that, we need some means of communicating intonation and stress, the sound of the speaking voice, which in itself, of course, is lost as we move from an oral to a visual medium. The pauses we use in speech, for example, to link some words together and to separate others from them are one of our most elementary and meaningful communicative devices. These pauses must be represented somehow on the printed or written page.

Clearly such things as spelling and punctuation take on great prominence in writing, whereas they do not exist at all in speech. Sure enough, we find that today these are two critical problem areas for student writers.

Learning to spell is largely a matter of training the visual memory. It is an even more basic skill than this book is designed to treat. As a writer you will learn very quickly that you may never outgrow your need to have a dictionary handy at all times, at least partly because you may never rely solely on your own memory for the spelling of all words.

Much of the second major section of this book does deal with ways in which the written page attempts to represent visually the speaking voice, and many matters treated there are related in one way or another to punctuation. As that section will seek to demonstrate at all times, such questions are not at all abstract matters of mere convention or outward "form"; they are basic issues that concern the simple communication of meaning, the essential task for any writer of "public language."

The student journalist has one great advantage over his or her contemporaries. As a writer for a printed medium, the journalist is at all times thinking of his or her writing as a distinctly visual form of communication. As we have seen, it is not always easy to do this in contemporary culture; the very nature of their writing task will help student journalists to *see* their thoughts written out before them rather than merely to hear or even just to "feel" them. This makes it easier for the journalist to make the necessary dual transition: from "personal" to "public" language, and from individual speech to impersonal printed writing.

THE BASICS ARE SIMPLE

Since we take ordinary communication so much for granted, we do not often think specifically about how it is accomplished. We are so busy concentrating upon the substance, the information or ideas, which we ourselves are articulating or are absorbing from others, that we are often not conscious of just *how* we are making ourselves understood or *how* we are understanding those other people. Learning to write, therefore, seems a rather peculiar enterprise, requiring a rather special way of looking at things. This is probably true even for professional writers like newspaper reporters or magazine feature writers. For them, too, so much attention is directed toward *what* is being communicated that *how* the communication is achieved is thought of, if at all, only when it causes a special problem. Thinking specifically about writing requires an unusual frame of mind.

But—and here is the important point—learning to write effectively is *not* particularly difficult. It may seem so at first, since paying attention to details of written language is so out of the ordinary. But the few basic guidelines for effective writing, including even those social norms of syntax and usage that may seem alien at first, are all very simple, very practical. They all arise from the everyday, pragmatic needs of people interacting together to accomplish the general business of social living. We do manage to get along in this difficult enterprise, somehow; we all could succeed at it better than we usually do. And one of the best ways to improve our ability to do so is to start improving our writing style.

The key factor we must recognize from the outset is that the efficient communication of information is primarily an impersonal, public, and social activity, accomplished in a written or printed medium. In order to improve our ability to write, therefore, we must learn to *see* our writing on the page as it will *look* to others who do not know us personally, and who are interested in *what* we are saying rather than in *who* we are.

Chapter II

THE SAMPLE CASE

CONTRASTING PROBLEMS: ONE

In the fall of 1974, an energetic, intelligent, self-confident young man—whom we shall call Roland—entered a large university in the East after a satisfying and rewarding career in high school. Among other subjects he signed up to take Composition, a required course for all incoming students in the College of Liberal Arts. Roland had not fully made up his mind, but he believed that eventually he was destined for a career in communications, which would probably be his major field of study in college. In chatting with his Composition instructor the first day of class, Roland happened to mention that he was particularly eager to do well in that course since he was looking forward to a possible career in journalism and especially since he had already had some experience along that line. He had been editor of the high-school newspaper in his senior year, after two years as a reporter and feature writer.

"I hope you're a tough grader," he told his professor. "My high-school adviser said you only learn from strict teachers."

Roland's self-assurance was in for a shock.

The first assignment I gave to Roland's class was to write a simple, one-page description of an object. I thought that would pose no problem whatever for a student journalist like Roland, the simple descriptive skill being (I presumed) the most basic tool of a reporter. My own composure was also due for a shock.

The essay Roland turned in simply did not make sense. Try as I might, with the best will in the world, I could not understand what Roland was trying to say, could not picture the object, could not

24

have identified it if I had seen it among other objects of the same general type. Roland's description was filled with what seemed to me the most elementary types of writing errors: misspelled words, sentence fragments, pronouns whose meaning I could not trace, verbs whose subjects I could not find, phrases that you would think no native speaker of the language could *say* without stammering and then "correcting" himself. All these bizarre phrases and sentences simply did not communicate any meaning.

The most elementary task of the informational writer was not achieved in this first little paper Roland handed in; the object he was describing remained as unknown to the reader, to me or to any other reader, after its description had been read as it had been beforehand.

Roland's case is perhaps extreme, but unfortunately, it is not untypical. He had indeed had considerable experience as a student journalist, but he had somehow failed to pick up some of the most fundamental skills necessary to that occupation. He was not an irresponsible person either—far from it. During that first semester in college he rewrote every paper assigned after it had been graded; sometimes he rewrote them more than once. He came in for regular individual conferences. He had friends read over his essays before handing them in. He kept a huge stack of notes both from the Composition course and from his own observation of his particular weaknesses as a writer.

As all this work was getting under way, I was still finding it a bit hard to believe that Roland had in fact been a publishing journalist for several years. When he offered to show me some of the stories he had written for his school paper, I was eager to look them over. Perhaps, I thought, the basic skills Roland clearly lacked had been provided by a conscientious editor. But what about the issues Roland himself had edited? Perhaps the sponsor of the newspaper had quietly "corrected" all the "errors," rewriting most of the stories? That did not seem very likely; it would have taken too much time!

This may have been the case, but the difference between the issues Roland had edited himself and the earlier issues in which his articles had appeared could still be seen. Here and there throughout the issues Roland had edited, several of those basic writing problems did appear, and as a result the *sense* the writer was apparently trying to communicate did not come through. Even in his own stories, which had obviously been carefully edited, sentences appeared that simply did not communicate anything.

The judges of a statewide competition among school newspapers in the Southwest have reported that such problems are not uncommon today. Roland's problems are apparently shared by many student journalists all over the country.

With hard work that first semester, Roland made remarkable progress. By the end he was writing adequately, and it was clear that he had made the most important step, which would allow him to improve from that point on merely with more and more experience. What he had had to learn, essentially, was that language communicates by means of conventional patterns: habitual ways of linking words together, modifying their form so that their precise relationships to each other are immediately clear to anyone who is also familiar with the usual habits. The person who wants to communicate not only clearly but also as rapidly as possible simply has to be thoroughly familiar with the language habits his or her readers will have established already.

Without these conventional patterns, which we often call "correct grammar," no written or printed use of language can communicate efficiently.

CONTRASTING PROBLEMS: TWO

Back in 1962, another young man signed up for a course in Expository Writing at his university in the Midwest. He was rather like Roland. Several years before, he too had been editor of his high-school paper after two years as a reporter and columnist. In addition, during the two years he had been in college, he had been taking courses in journalism and had been writing regularly for the campus newspaper. He had even worked one summer for a commercial daily newspaper in his hometown. He had been writing the sportscasts and announcing classical music for the campus radio station for more than a year.

Like Roland later, this young fellow was about to discover that, despite his experience, he still had a lot to learn about writing effectively.

I had better say without further ado that this second case is my own. Yes, I know that rude shock firsthand!

Looking back, I guess I must have been pretty sure of myself as I signed up for Expository Writing. I was a second-semester sophomore in college, making fairly good grades. I felt especially confident of my ability to write. I knew that anyone can always improve his writing, but I thought that I needed just a little polishing up on the finer points of stylistic excellence. Basically, I felt sure, my writing was even more communicative, more meaningful than most other people's. My experience as a reporter and radio announcer had helped give me this exaggerated confidence in my writing ability.

You may not be surprised to learn that my first assignment in the Expository Writing class was to describe a simple object. I described a door. My essay took up three and a half pages. ("A piece of cake," I said to myself, handing it in.)

The graduate student who marked that paper gave it back a few days later without a grade. It was so bad, he said, it didn't even deserve an *F!* Of the three and a half pages, he had scratched a huge X through all but the first paragraph. Instead of a grade, he wrote a two-word comment: *Meaningless verbiage.*

Now, that was cruel. A sincere student's feelings should not be trampled upon that way. But the truth of the matter is, of course, that the grader was right.

INTERPRETING CASES ONE AND TWO

Roland's "case" and my own are exact opposites. Effective writing lies somewhere between these two extremes. Roland's writing at first lacked the conventional patterns out of which any meaningful language (spoken or written) is made. My own student writing was quite different. It is true that it did not contain any obvious "grammatical errors." All my sentences were complete. All the pronouns did what they were supposed to do. All subjects matched their verbs adequately.

My writing, you see, was indeed sufficiently conventional; all those habitual patterns necessary for communication were right where they should have been. *But they were almost empty of meaning!* As we shall see and as I had to learn "the hard way" myself, "grammatical correctness" is not enough to insure effective writing that communicates information clearly and rapidly. What I had to learn was to scrutinize carefully each of my sentences, each phrase, each word, considering precisely what was the specific, concrete meaning I intended to communicate by means of those words. I had to find those places in my writing in which I had written a "correct" pattern that sounded good but that was not really significant. I had to learn to eliminate those instances of "meaningless verbiage."

EXAMPLES OF INEFFECTIVE COMMUNICATION

These days, high-school and college teachers seem to agree that the most prevalent problems young writers are encountering are more like Roland's than like my own twelve years earlier, though either weakness can make a person's writing ineffective. The habitual patterns of "correctness," without which no use of language can communicate efficiently, are apparently not very clearly recognized by young writers today, or at least they are often not clearly represented to the eye on the pages these students have written.

Sometimes, merely correcting the obvious errors in grammar and punctuation does not make the written work much more communicative. But if the patterns are put right, perhaps the problems of "making sense" will be immediately evident even to the writer.

Here is a little description of a chair, given to me by a student journalist last year. What I am quoting represents the third revision of the original, which was itself marked by many basic errors in spelling, punctuation, agreement of subject and verb, and that sort of thing. With those errors eliminated, the description reads fairly well, unless you study it closely.

The Chair

Furniture serves as an instrument to sit, read, sleep, and watch television, among other things. One item of furniture that is used frequently is the chair.

The chair is two feet in height. The back and the legs are metal. The seat is red, and it is made out of a vinyl.

The chair has rectangular legs that are formed by two long thick pieces of metal. The metal is molded into the form of a horseshoe. This is done to enable the chair to stand. Connected by metal screws on the bottom of the legs are small round discs that are also made out of metal. The discs balance the chair.

The seat has two metal screws drilled through its legs on both sides for stability. The seat is square, fourteen inches on all four sides.

The back of the chair is adjacent to another red vinyl cushion. This is supported by one continuous piece of thick metal, five feet long. The cushion is shaped in a half-moon. Two screws on each side of the cushion are drilled through the metal to secure the seat to the back of the chair.

The legs and the back rest of the chair are soldered together at the intersection of the legs and the back support. This is done to maintain its stability so it will not fall apart.

A simple description like this, presented as an essay, always looks a little silly. Beginnings and endings seem particularly awkward or abrupt. That is not the thing to notice here, however. Ignoring the mindlessness of the assignment, we might say that this piece now reads pretty well, fairly smoothly and conventionally. On the surface, for instance, there is nothing "'wrong" with the following sentence from the next-to-last paragraph:

The back of the chair is adjacent to another red vinyl cushion.

The grammar here is conventional; all the spelling is normal. Read aloud, the sentence sounds all right.

But what does it mean?

If we look carefully at this sentence, I believe we will see that it does not *say* very much. The words "adjacent to" are not precise enough. The "back of the chair" might be *at the side* of this other "red vinyl cushion," or it might be *above* it, or even *below* it. We might expect from the context that the writer meant the back of the chair "rises vertically from a second, horizontal red vinyl cushion, which forms the seat."

But if that is the intended meaning, what does the next sentence mean?

This [cushion] is supported by one continuous piece of thick metal, five feet long.

A "chair" whose "seat" is *five feet long?* Perhaps the writer means "five feet *wide,*" but if so, isn't this something like a "bench" and not a chair at all? Then again, perhaps he means "five feet *high*" or "tall." Is this a "high chair" or a "bar stool" perhaps?

How difficult this business of communicating simple information may turn out to be after all!

Notice also the last sentence of the same paragraph:

> Two screws on each side of the cushion are drilled through the metal . . .

How does one "drill a screw through metal"? This cannot have been what the writer intended to say; but it *is* what his words mean.

And of course, I suppose everyone noticed that the first sentence says that pieces of furniture actually "watch television, among other things." I wonder what "other things" besides television this writer thinks pieces of furniture do "watch." Also, I wonder what their favorite programs are!

Here is a more serious example, typical of the kind of fundamental problems appearing in the essays and articles written by young people finishing high school today. In order to illustrate in one of her essays that the richest families are not necessarily the happiest, a young woman wrote about a meaningful experience of her own. I reproduce this passage exactly as it was turned in to me, with only the most obvious and distracting typographical errors removed:

> The day continues on and I saw many men get drunk, many wives get angry, and many children cry.
>
> The whole idea of the picnic was what I felt a good idea. To bring these people and their families together for a day and have a good time. It was the end of the summer, so it was like a finale of the summer. At least it seemed that way for me.
>
> The people at the picnic were what interested me the most. I was brought up in what is considered in my home town, a middle class family. (above the tracks, but not to high up) In what I've seen of middle class families in my neighborhood is that anything that is done, is not done as a family. Each does "their own thing." The only get togethers are on hoildays, which everyone hates and winds up tolerating each other. These families are basically finically stable, and this is what keeps them together.
>
> It made me happy to see all these families together, doing something they enjoyed. They were enjoying being with each other.
>
> These people, who I always believed to be so "pig headed" with

their bigotedness are just that. However, maybe no more pig-headed than I am about them. They live in situations where if the families don't pull together real tight the people in the families can very easily fall to peices because of their financial status. Their love for each other is what really leeps them together.

This makes me wonder if it's better to have money or love. That statement may seem somewhat misleading, I wonder if it's always one way or the other, or if it's possible to have both.

With a little imagination and sensitivity, we can understand fairly well the general sentiment being expressed here. And it seems to me an important point, which the writer apparently felt rather strongly about. The disarming simplicity of this statement—

This makes me wonder if it's better to have money or love.

—particularly strikes home.

But it seems such a shame for an important point, strongly felt, to be only *fairly* well communicated, *generally* understood, and even that only after the reader has had to work on the passage exercising his or her own imagination and sensitivity. If the reader has to think about it, trying to infer something not explicit in the language at first glance, his or her attention is being drawn away from the information or ideas being expressed and toward the manner in which they are expressed and the person who is expressing them.

Such may be the function of literary art, but not of public language designed primarily to communicate information clearly and succinctly. And besides, I doubt that anyone could feel that the passage quoted here, despite its apparent sincerity, is "artistic" in any meaningful sense. The spelling and typing errors are acutely distressing; how can we read the following sentence with the sympathy it deserves?

Their love for each other is what really leeps them together.

Of course, we know that the intention was to write *keeps* instead of *leeps*. But the typing error by itself distracts our attention to some degree, no matter how hard we are trying to think about only the idea or feelings the writer intended to communicate.

But there are more basic problems throughout this little piece, which even more certainly prevent it from communicating effectively. Let us look closely at the third paragraph, with all its spelling and typographical errors corrected:

> The people at the picnic were what interested me the most. I was brought up in what is considered in my hometown, a middle-class family. (above the tracks, but not too high up) In what I have seen of middle-class families in my neighborhood is that anything that is done, is not done as a family. Each does "their own thing." The only get-togethers are on holidays, which everyone hates and winds up tolerating each other. These families are basically financially stable, and this is what keeps them together.

(In case anyone is counting, this represents ten corrections.)

I wonder if this passage read aloud would communicate satisfactorily. Surely at least part of the problem is the writer's having inadequately translated her basically oral thought to the visual page. By controlling her emphasis and pace in speech, the student could properly render what should be the second sentence here:

I was brought up in what is considered, in my hometown, a middle-class family (above the tracks, but not too high up).

But the next sentence would not make sense no matter how it was read:

In what I have seen . . . is that . . .

This combination of linking words simply does not conform to the basic ways in which the American English language carries meaning. You would think that no native speaker of that language could leave such a "sentence" unrevised, whether speaking *or* writing. You and I are not in the best position to attempt such a revision. Only the writer herself can decide what she means here. But perhaps we can speculate. It is hard work, trying to make the thought precise and trying to get the words on the page to represent it with equal precision. Is this a sufficient improvement?

Original: In what I have seen of middle-class families in my neighborhood is that anything that is done is not done as a family.

Revised: According to what I have seen of the middle-class families in my neighborhood, whatever they do is not done as a family.

(1) Adding *the* before "'middle-class families" is easy, and it does help make the phrase more precise, tying it more closely together.

(2) Changing "'anything that is done" to *whatever they do* also seems to me a considerable improvement, eliminating the vagueness in the passive verb—which is not intended—but leaving the generality of "anything," which seems essential to the intended meaning.

(3) Changing the first word "'in" to *according to* may seem like a minor adjustment, but it is in fact the most significant change in the whole revision. Together with eliminating "is that," revising the opening preposition here completely alters the way the words (or thoughts) are related to each other.

Pushing on, let us examine the next two sentences:

Each does "their own thing." The only get-togethers are on holidays, which everyone hates and winds up tolerating each other.

The first sentence probably makes its point all right, although it surely contains a potentially misleading shift from the singular *each* to the plural *their*. But the last half of the next sentence again just does not make sense.

Perhaps here, too, there may be a problem with moving from speech to writing. In speaking, perhaps, we might sometimes forget how our longer sentences have begun and end them with makeshift phrasing that might make a wholly new point. Do you see that the problem with the last of this sentence is that the *verb* "winds up" has no *subject?*

. . . which everyone hates and winds up tolerating each other.

The writer, we may assume, intended for *everyone* to be the subject of *winds up.* Perhaps in speaking she could have emphasized this word in some way that would have made her intention clear (though I do not see how, frankly). In any case, it does not come through that way on the page. To the eye, consciously or unconsciously, it would seem that the words following *which everyone hates and* . . . will have exactly the same pattern as *everyone hates:* subject + verb (with *which* functioning as an implied object).

Maybe the whole sentence should be rethought. The only way one might revise it in its present form would be to make it clear, on the visual page, that the last part of the sentence has a different pattern from the phrase just before:

> The only get-togethers are on holidays, which everyone hates and at which everyone winds up [merely] tolerating each other.

The last sentence of this paragraph and the first of the next one together produce a profound confusion, which makes it quite impossible to understand the passage without considerable effort on the part of the reader:

> These families are basically financially stable, and this is what keeps them together.
> It made me happy to see all these families together . . .

"These families" in the first sentence are *not the same* in the writer's mind as "these families" in the next sentence. How is that crucial fact communicated? *Is* it communicated?

Like prepositions and sentence structure, pronouns such as *these* are essential means by which the links among thoughts are made clear. The same phrase cannot refer to two different thoughts, or things, without producing gross confusion.

With that ambiguity resolved and with the emphasis slightly modified, these two sentences can be revised so as to give us, as a whole, the following version of the passage we have been considering. It does seem much improved, not only in "outward form" but in the degree to which it communicates effectively:

> The people at the picnic were what interested me the most. I was brought up in what is considered, in my hometown, a middle-class family (above the tracks, but not too high up). According to what I have seen of the middle-class families in my neighborhood, what-

ever they do is not done as a family. Each member of the family "does his own thing." The only get-togethers are on holidays, which everyone hates and at which everyone winds up tolerating each other. Middle-class families are basically stable financially, and this is what keeps them together.

It made me happy the day of the picnic to see all these other families together . . .

Your Own "Case"

I hope it will seem to all the student writers who are reading this book that the problems we have been discussing in this chapter are much more elementary than they would ever find in their own writing. But I must warn you that, if you are a typical student journalist in the mid-1970's, you are likely to have to struggle quite a bit with just this sort of writing problem.

This should not seem sufficient cause for either resentment or guilt on the young writer's part. It is a problem that naturally arises in a culture, like ours, which is moving away from a print-dominated, fairly coherent order toward one that still includes a serious need for visual, verbal communication skills but incorporates that need within a larger, more complex structure.

It may seem like hard work, as I suggested, revising your writing so that it does communicate efficiently and clearly. But the basic principles by which the revisions should be made are relatively simple to learn. Putting them into practice is hard at first, but it becomes easier and easier with extended, practical experience.

Chapter III

LEARNING TO SEE YOUR WRITING

The first and most essential step in learning to write well requires an act of the imagination. Every time you write an article or a feature, and particularly every time you revise your first draft, you must imagine someone whom you do not know in the process of reading what you have written.

Again, the journalist has a distinct advantage over his or her fellow writers in this respect, since a journalist's writing is thought of, from the first, as eventually *being read* by The General Public. The publishing writer's imagination, in other words, is grounded securely in the simple facts of his or her profession. Imagining a nameless *reader* looking at the words and other symbols he or she has put down on paper should not be quite so hard for the journalist as it might be for other writers. But it still requires imagination.

WHAT THE READER SEES

As a writer of this sort, you have the goal of communicating quickly and clearly information that you know to anyone (or everyone) who does not know it. A moment's thought should be enough to reveal that, from your reader's perspective, those marks you are responsible for on the written or printed page are *all there is*. The visual page and only the visual page must do the job of communicating your information.

Consider for a moment all the communicative devices the writer of this sort does *not* have. Of course, since no one is literally "speaking" the written or printed words and sentences, we do not have the sound of a person's voice placing emphasis, controlling pace and thus grouping and separating various clumps of words, or implying various attitudes by intonation. Likewise in printed or written communication we have no gestures by the hands, head, or shoulders, no facial expressions, to help control meaning. We have at most, in fact, only a minimal sense of "personality" in this kind of writing, as we have seen.

Furthermore, in most instances of written communication, no fixed context helps to inform the meaning of the words and sentences themselves. There is surely no interpersonal relationship between the writer and his audience, which might help the reader to understand what the writer intends to communicate. For most articles in newspapers and magazines (or on radio or television news shows, for that matter), no even purely informational context exists that might inform the individual story either; most such articles are self-contained, unrelated to the ones coming before or after, or appearing around them.

The printed words and sentences alone must be sufficient to carry your meaning to the reader.

If everything necessary for efficient, unambiguous communication *fails* to appear on the page in this sort of writing, the results may not absolutely prevent communication. Consider this example adapted from a college newspaper:

A *Daily Bugle* poll of 250 students indicates that plagiarism a problem at State.

I expect you can spot the oversight in this sentence immediately. "Plagiarism *is* a problem," it should read. The word *is* has been left out, and the normal, expected patterns of language by which English words come to have meaning are not represented in this passage.

On the other hand, I doubt that this particular oversight would cause too much difficulty. The reader would probably understand the sentence immediately despite the essential word-omission. (You can never be certain, however, that such an unconventional pattern will communicate effectively.)

The same problem can easily cause more basic difficulties:

Leading participants in the most recent confrontation were Maj. Gen. Thomas R. Murphy, Deputy Commander of the local base, and Randolph Jackson, President of the Truman High Student Council. When Gen. <u>Murphy arrived on the scene yesterday, would not stay.</u> Wishing to "cool things off," as he later said, he departed immediately.

The writer of the sentence above about "plagiarism" might feel that an editor or even a proofreader could easily correct his or her error, filling in the little word left out. In this longer example, however, which I have adapted from an essay by one of my recent students, no one but the writer could know what the underlined sentence is intended to mean. Was it the Deputy Commander who left, or was it the Student Council President? The context does not make this crucial information clear; and of course, the sentence itself—with the subject of its verb *would not stay* simply missing—does not do so either. This is not a mere matter of "neatness" or "proofreading." It is a failure to communicate essential information.

What the Writer Sees

We can be relatively certain that the writer of neither of these two stories had actually made a "grammatical error." Leaving out the verb of the one sentence and the subject of the other were undoubtedly what each writer would consider "merely" a slip in translating what he or she had thought into what was actually written. From the writer's perspective, it may even have been "merely" a typing error.

But in writing that is primarily designed to communicate information efficiently, it is not the writer's perspective that matters the most. In a sense, it is the reader's perspective that matters most. The goal is communication; the means by which that goal is accomplished, if at all, are the visible marks on the written or printed page. What the reader sees, therefore, is the sole material cause of what she or he understands.

We have considered some of the communicative devices that the writer does not have at his or her disposal. Consider as well that the writer of this kind of communication does not have any knowledge of his or her audience. In most cases when we are talking, we can sense immediately how well we are communicating by observing our audience's reactions to our words, by noting *their* gestures, facial expressions, and so on. In written or printed communication of information, however, just as the writer is not observable by the reader, so is the reader invisible to the writer. All that is necessary for the anonymous, silent writer to communicate his or her information to the invisible, impersonal reader must be right there on the visual page.

TRAINING THE WRITER'S EYE

Noticing the visual aspects of writing is quite an unusual activity. Normally, when we are reading for information we are concentrating so much on what seems the "content" of the written or printed language that we do not pay any attention to the means by which it is being communicated. Minor slips, such as that word *is* inadvertently left out of the first sentence we looked at a few pages back, might go by totally unnoticed. The meaning is all we are usually interested in, and since the meaning in such a case might be quite clear, we may not even *see* that the visible marks on the page do not "say" precisely what we understand as we are reading them. Even professional journalists, when they are reading someone else's newspaper or magazine, may not always attend consciously to the visual aspects of the writing. They, too, may be concentrating on *what* is being communicated so much that they might not even notice *how* the communication is being achieved.

An informational writer is also primarily interested in *what* she or he has to "say." Like the reader's, the writer's mind may be focused mainly upon the information to be communicated. *The crucial difference is that the writer cannot afford to ignore the visual aspect of his or her writing, as the reader can.* It is the writer's job to make sure that the visual symbols he or she is responsible for are enough, by themselves, to convey the intended information.

Since paying attention to the visible side of informational writing may indeed be such a peculiar exercise, but nevertheless a necessary one for the writer, it may take some special training. Writers must be able to *see* what they have written on the pages that they are eventually going to submit to a reader. This requires a special ability in eye control.

Notice how the focus of your eyes is moving across this very page, grouping some words together, separating others from those around them, in order to shape meaningful clusters and in this way to comprehend the sense I am trying to communicate to you.

See what happens?

Your attention does not move, as you may have thought, in a smooth, continuous, or regular flow from one side of the page to the other, but instead jumps ahead, pauses and absorbs, and then jumps again. Let's look at that sentence once more, exaggerating its visual aspects:

Notice how . . .

This, I would guess, is the first unit the reader attends to. Then there would follow a slight gap before the next unit.

Notice how   *the focus of your eyes*   is . . .

And so it goes, as the reader's mind shapes those marks on the page into groups of words, and eventually into sentences that "make sense," that have or communicate meaning.

Notice how   the focus of your eyes
        is   moving   across this very page
            grouping some words together
                separating others   from those around them
        in order   to shape   meaningful clusters
            and   in this way
    to comprehend the sense   I am trying   to communicate to you.

Even this broken-up representation of the reading process is far less complex than what actually happens. And besides, what actually happens is probably slightly different for each person and for each time he or she reads.

But I wonder if the general point is clear: do you see that what happens as a continuous passage of ordinary prose is being read is that the words are clumped together and separated from the others around them so that units of meaning are created?

Do you see also that those units of meaning are the very ones that might be created by grouping and separating words *in speech?*

And do you see, finally, that although the reader's eyes and mind can change the visible symbols quite a bit so that the meaning apparently inherent in the words can be understood, the writer must also give the reader some extra, visual signs in order to help the reader group some things together and separate others?

For instance, the capital *N* at the beginning (and the white space above and beside it that marks the paragraph) helps separate this large unit, the sentence, from everything else. In speech this would be done by a relatively long pause, which would emphasize what finally is pronounced.

Each word, of course, is separated from the others by a space. In speech most words in the same sentence or phrase are not separated by pauses, but each is emphasized "separately" in one way or another by the way the sentence is pronounced.

And finally, yes, punctuation marks appear here also, separating some groups of words from others and thus reproducing the pauses that a person would *hear* if this sentence were being *spoken*. The commas separate each group from every other group, and the period separates the whole unit from everything around it.

In conversation we pronounce and hear such pauses and stresses. In written or printed communication we must see them.

READING ALOUD

Since the writer's essential task might be thought of as the "translation" of speech into visible signs, it may be a useful exercise for the young writer to reverse the process. What the writer needs to understand and to be fully conscious of is just *how* we ordinarily make the printed or written page correlate with the speaking voice. Perhaps a good way to start thinking about this correlation between speaking in order to communicate information and writing or printing would be to demonstrate to yourself that you already know the basic principles by which our society has decided to make the transition from speech to writing. Just make the same transition in the opposite direction, moving from writing back to speech!

Try reading the following passage aloud, paying attention to two different things. Notice, of course, *what* you are saying; or in other words, do not fail to notice the meaning of the passage. But at the same time, notice the particular visual signs on the printed page that cause you to vary the *way* you are speaking: your reading speed, your emphasis, and so on. Maybe it will take two separate readings, both aloud, for you to notice each of these two things. (Incidentally, I have adapted this passage from a story in the high-school newspaper I helped to edit back in 1959–60.)

Drama Club News

"I Remember Mama," a play adapted from Kathryn Forbes' novel *Mama's Bank Account,* will be presented Nov. 1 and 2 in the Whitfield Auditorium as the Drama Club's first production of the year.

Narrated by Eileen Martin, who portrays Katrina, the eldest daughter of the Nelson family, the drama depicts the heartaches and happiness of a Norwegian family living in San Francisco in the 1920's. Mama, played by June Marshall, is a sensitive, warm-hearted person who instills calm in the rest of the family during periods of strife.

Tom Hill portrays Papa in this Drama Club presentation, and Richard Montgomery plays his son. A younger daughter, Christine, portrayed by Marta Eastlake, and Dagmar, the youngest child, played by Sue Johnson, bring Mama more than their share of family trouble. . . .

When this passage is spoken in such a way that the information in it is successfully conveyed to anyone who might hear, the voice of the speaker must translate into sound not only the letters constituting all the words represented. That is one thing, but a good many other things are almost equally essential in order to turn this visual passage into spoken communication.

For instance, notice how differently you would pronounce the opening three words if you were talking about your own memory of your own mother: "I remember Mama," you would say in a certain tone, which would probably emphasize in one way or another the mental act of your memory that would be communicated in the word *remember*. But when we see on the page

"I Remember Mama," a play . . .

and read that aloud, we pronounce those very same words quite differently. We have to say those words in a special way, so that our listener will not think that we are talking about actually remembering our mother but that we are giving a title instead. In other words, probably by running all the words together and emphasizing them all equally, we say

"I Remember Mama," a play . . .

instead of saying

I remember Mama. A play . . .

The quotation marks and the capitalization of each word in the title are translated in speech into a certain intonation and talking speed, so that the meaning—a particular play's title, not an act of memory—is communicated. The visual signs are the printed indication of this meaning, which would be indicated in other ways in speech. (A similar thing happens, of course, with the novel title *Mama's Bank Account*. There, too, what is seen as punctuation has a special meaning just as a certain way of speaking the title has a specific meaning when we read that passage aloud.)

The other punctuation marks here—the commas and periods, and the breaks between paragraphs—would also be "heard" by someone listening to you read this passage aloud. They would all be translated from visual signs into pauses of varying lengths. Just where they appear, of course, shapes the basic meaning of the passage.

Notice how the meaning of the following section, for example, could be changed simply by moving the most significant pause:

. . . The drama depicts the heartaches and happiness of a Norwegian family living in San Francisco in the 1920's. Mama, played by June Marshall, is . . .

When you read this aloud a moment ago, your longest pause corresponded to the period, the blank spaces, and the capital letter visible on the printed page between the words *1920's* and *Mama*.

What if a person were to read the same passage aloud, pausing for the longest time instead between the words *family* and *living?* Do you see? The meaning of the two sentences would be changed, changed in a way that would be normally represented visually like this:

. . . The drama depicts the heartaches and happiness of a Norwegian family. Living in San Francisco in the 1920's, Mama, played by June Marshall, is . . .

Printed or pronounced in this second way, the passage means something different from what the original passage meant. Not *the family* but only *Mama* is said now to be "living in San Francisco in the 1920's." As we read this part of the modified passage, we do not know where or when the family as a whole lived.

Notice also that the commas appearing in the printed story would have the sound in speech of varying lengths of silence. A comma is clearly the visible sign of a pause in speech, but the length of the pause may be relatively short or relatively long, depending on the meaning of the sentence. In the first part of the sentence we have been looking at, for example, three commas appear:

> Narrated by Eileen Martin, who portrays Katrina, the eldest daughter of the Nelson family, the drama depicts . . .

Each of the commas, when the passage is read aloud, becomes a pause of a different length. The pause after *Eileen Martin* is fairly significant; the words *narrated by Eileen Martin* at the very beginning have to be pronounced in such a way that they will be remembered when the words *the drama* are pronounced quite a bit later. If these words are not "put together" by the sound of the speaker's voice, the passage will not make sense.

> Narrated by Eileen Martin——the drama depicts . . .

The second pause, which follows *Katrina,* is relatively short when this passage is read aloud:

> Narrated by Eileen Martin, who portrays <u>Katrina, the eldest daughter</u> of the Nelson family. . . .

If the pause after *Katrina* were too long, the meaning of the passage would be changed: the listener would think that "Eileen Martin" was "the eldest daughter" referred to. This clearly is not true; Katrina is the daughter. Once again, there is a particular correlation that must be made between the visual and the spoken sentence, if the same meaning is to be communicated.

The final pause, following *family,* is the longest of these three:

> Narrated by Eileen Martin, who portrays Katrina, the eldest daughter of the Nelson <u>family, the drama</u> depicts . . .

The words *the drama* have to be dissociated fairly sharply from *the Nelson family* so that the listener can remember the related words *Narrated by Eileen Martin* from the beginning of the sentence. I do not believe it is possible for the last words—

daughter of the Nelson family the drama depicts . . .

—to be pronounced in this sentence with no pause after *family* in a way that still makes sense. The pause that comma represents seems essential to the meaning of the sentence.

The purpose of reading a passage like this aloud, it should be remembered, is not to make you acquainted (or enamored) with the sound of your own voice. It is to help you become conscious of how visual signs on the printed or written page are communicative devices just like the stresses, pauses, and intonations you use in speech every day.

TWO MORE SAMPLE PASSAGES

If such an exercise is useful once, maybe it will be useful twice or even three times. Here are two more passages of informational writing that you may want to read aloud. Bear in mind as you do so that your goal is to pay attention to the correlation between the printed signs and the variations in your speaking voice. Bear in mind also that the purpose you are pretending to have in "speaking" this passage is to communicate the information implicit in the author's words. You are not, as a radio announcer may have to do sometimes, simply filling in "dead air" or blotting out the silence. You are not lulling your listener to sleep with the mellifluous sound of your voice. You are telling her or him something that you assume is worth knowing, communicating information as a good newspaper or magazine reporter would do in print.

One of the most famous series of magazine features in American literature was written by Mark Twain. When it later appeared in book form, it was called *Life on the Mississippi,* and it began this way:

The Mississippi is well worth reading about. It is not a commonplace river, but on the contrary is in all ways remarkable. Considering the Missouri its main branch, it is the longest river in the world—four thousand three hundred miles. It seems safe to say that it is also the crookedest river in the world, since in one part of its journey it uses up one thousand three hundred miles to cover the same ground that the crow would fly over in six hundred and seventy-five. It discharges three times as much water as the St. Lawrence, twenty-five times as much as the Rhine, and three hundred and thirty-eight times as much as the Thames. No other river has so vast a drainage-basin; it draws its water-supply from twenty-eight states and territories; from Delaware on the Atlantic seaboard, and from all the country between that and Idaho on the Pacific slope—a spread of forty-five degrees of longitude. The Mississippi receives and carries to the Gulf water from fifty-four subordinate rivers that are navigable by steamboats, and from some hundreds that are navigable by flats and keels. The area of its drainage-basin is as great as the combined areas of England, Wales, Scotland, Ireland, France, Spain, Portugal, Germany, Austria, Italy, and Turkey; and almost all this wide region is fertile; the Mississippi valley, proper, is exceptionally so.

It is a remarkable river in this: that instead of widening toward its mouth, it grows narrower; grows narrower and deeper. From the junction of the Ohio to a point half-way down to the sea, the width averages a mile in high water; thence to the sea the width steadily diminishes, until, at the "Passes," above the mouth, it is but little over half a mile. At the junction of the Ohio the Mississippi's depth is eighty-seven feet; the depth increases gradually, reaching one hundred and twenty-nine just above the mouth . . .

This passage from Twain introduces us to four new punctuation marks: the hyphen (-), the dash (—), the semicolon (;), and the colon (:). The hyphen is really a spelling device, used to merge two words that could remain separate into a single word with a particular meaning of its own; e.g., *twenty-five* instead of *twenty* and *five*. As this passage suggests, the dash, the semicolon, and the colon all are the visual signs of what, in informative speaking, would be relatively long pauses, but not quite so long as most periods represent.

You may want to see whether or not this is indeed the way you "pronounced" those sentences in the Twain passage, and also to speculate about why each is used in its particular place instead of a simple comma.

Another section worth examining in detail for the way its visual signs correlate with the speaking voice is this one:

The Mississippi receives and <u>carries to the Gulf water from fifty-four subordinate rivers that are navigable by steamboats, and from</u> some hundreds that are navigable by flats and keels. The area of its drainage-basin is as great as the combined areas of England, Wales . . .

If you had been the writer of this passage, making the transition from what might be communicative speech to writing instead of reversing the movement as we have been doing, you might have been tempted to place a comma between *Gulf* and *water*. Can you "hear" why? One does indeed pause between those two words; it is necessary to do so to communicate the meaning desired. But a pause between the main elements of a sentence—between subject and verb or, as here, between verb and object—especially when the first element is relatively long in itself, is so very common in our language that marking the pause with visible punctuation is not necessary. (Since it would be unusual to do so, in fact, it might even be misleading.)

Here is a final passage you may want to read aloud, attending to how *saying* such a passage correlates with the visual signs on the printed page. (Again, I have adapted this story from my old school paper.)

Babble-On

If a visitor from outer space had dropped into the house at 1515 South Street last Friday between 7:30 and 10 P.M., he would have found it difficult to locate himself in Earth time and space.

Judging from the clothes of the various people he saw around him, he might have guessed he was anywhere from ancient Rome to Tzarist Russia or modern France. The speech he would have heard could not have solved his puzzle, since the strangely clad folk spoke jumbled mixtures of English, German, Spanish, French, Russian, and even Latin.

Our interplanetary traveler would have found himself at the annual "International Festival," sponsored by the language clubs and departments of Senior High.

Held this year under the direction of Le Cercle Français (the French club), sponsored by Mme. Helene Bouquin, the party gathered at the home of sophomore Vic Meirgarten. All language club members were invited to attend, wearing the garb of the country where their language is spoken. . . .

Notice the special, lowered tone of voice that a speaker of this passage would use in pronouncing the words "the French club" between slight pauses. These pauses and this lowered tone are the meaning of the parentheses around those words.

Note also that the slight pause between "Our interplanetary traveler" and "would have found himself" is not marked by any punctuation, because it represents a very brief interruption between subject and verb, the main elements in the sentence.

THE VALUE OF READING ALOUD

Reading printed passages aloud, taking care both to communicate their meaning orally and to notice just how their meaning is made visible on the page, may help to train your eye to *see* the communicative devices used in writing or printing. Reading your own writing aloud may help you to *imagine* someone else in the process of reading what you have written. A journalist must be able to do both these things.

Some young writers find it very helpful to read their own first drafts aloud to someone else as an aid in revision. This may help them to imagine someone else reading their writing, and it may help them to insure that the visual signs they have put on the page are all that is indeed necessary for effective communication. It seems probable that, for some writers, reading aloud would help eliminate what to a reader would seem either to make no sense or to be a simpleminded error. I find it hard to believe, for example, that any native speaker of our language could "say" the following sentence, from our Sample Case in Chapter II, without knowing something was seriously wrong with it:

> Furniture serves as an instrument to sit, read, sleep, and watch television, among other things.

I suppose that sentence might "look" all right to a casual glance; but I cannot imagine that it could *sound* all right if read aloud.

The same is perhaps true of what a writer might be tempted to think of as "merely typing errors." It is possible that reading aloud might help some writers *see* what visual signs they have left on the page, such as this sentence:

The day continues on, and I saw many men get drunk.

For the reader, this represents a peculiar and misleading change in the verb tense: the present *continues* for no apparent reason is exchanged for the past *saw*. From the writer's perspective, this may well have been merely a typing error, substituting *s* for *d* in what should have been *continued*. But as we have seen, in writing designed primarily to communicate information clearly and rapidly it is not the writer's perspective that matters the most. The writing or printing on the page must accurately represent visibly what the writer intends to say.

A word of caution may be in order here, however. There is a limit to the value of reading your writing aloud. Such an exercise is one way to make yourself conscious of the visual aspects of communicative writing and to help you to imagine a reader seeing the marks you have put on the page. But two dangers may arise for some writers (I am one of them myself, incidentally). First, since you already know what you intend for the writing to say, you may think you see something on the page that you have not actually put there. In reading the passage aloud, you may rely on the tone of your voice, on gestures or facial expressions, to communicate what in the final account must be communicated solely by the words and other marks visible on the page itself.

Remember, if you attempt this revision aid, that its purpose is to *slow your eye down* and to *help you see clearly*. If you find that it works in the opposite direction for you personally, if you are "blinded" by the sound of your voice, then find some other way to slow your eye down and help you see your writing. (Many writers hold a blank sheet of paper so that it covers up all but a phrase at a time as they read through what they have written.)

Another danger in reading your own writing aloud is that it is definitely possible for language to "sound good" that does not *say* or communicate anything. Just because a sentence "sounds" pleasant to the ear does not mean that it is effective writing; it may be "meaningless verbiage," you know.

The reverse, however, probably is a reliable guide: if a sentence you have written does *not* sound good, chances are that indeed something is wrong with it. Even if you are unable to spot precisely what the "error" is in such an instance, it is usually wise to rewrite a sentence that does not sound right, starting all over again on a blank line.

Bear in mind at all times that the purpose of all such exercises is to make the writer consciously aware of the visual aspect of his or her occupation. Since the reader will understand only what the visible marks on the page communicate to her or him, the writer must make certain that those visual signs are precisely what he or she intended and exactly what is needed for effective communication to take place.

Seeing Language in an Oral Culture

Writing is visual; speaking is oral and aural; *thinking* seems prior to both writing and speaking and seems neither visual nor oral. Communication would seem to be a means of letting someone else understand what you are thinking. If you have information to communicate, you might communicate it in speech: in which case, you would have a great many devices at your disposal —the words themselves, pauses and stresses, gestures, tones, facial expressions, and so on. But as a communicative *writer,* you have at your disposal only the *visual* signs you make on the page before you.

For a journalist, who from the outset thinks of his or her communication as public and probably printed, it should not be too difficult to get used to the need to *look at* what she or he has written. But in a society that was once, but is no longer, dominated by the visual, verbal communications media, even a journalist may have to make a special effort. After the need is clearly understood, the effort is really minimal. All it takes is a little conscious effort at first, a little experience thinking about what writing or printing "looks like" and how it correlates with speech, and then the necessary habits will be formed. After a while most writers *see* their writing without having to think about it.

LOOK CAREFULLY WHAT YOU WRITE!
LEARN TO SEE WHAT WRITTEN ON THE PAGE!

(Get the point?)

PART 2

Correctness

Chapter IV

A HIERARCHY OF WRITING FLAWS

In the 1950's, students of language finally seemed to communicate to the "English teachers" of this country one of their first discoveries, from more than a century before, about the basic nature of all languages. For the past twenty years or so, not only professional linguists but also teachers of writing and literature, and even the general public, have understood fairly well that every language in actual use is in a constant process of change. The language we speak and write is always adapting to changing needs and circumstances.

The significant implication of this fact for students and teachers of writing seemed clear at first: if our language is constantly changing, then there can be no fixed rules about how the language should be used. Evidently, you cannot call a particular use of language "correct" or "incorrect"; the best you can do is speculate about whether or not it is "appropriate" to its particular "situation." General standards of "correctness" in grammar and word choice, it might seem, are really only temporary and perhaps even class-defined "prejudices." It seems misleading to call anyone's use of language an "error" or (as I say above) a "flaw."

Now it is certainly true, as we have seen, that moral and even political issues do inevitably surround questions of language usage. Languages are always changing, and besides that, in different circumstances the very same person uses several slightly different languages. You do talk differently to your friends, for example, than to people you do not know personally, don't you? Rather than seeking general standards that apply universally to "correct usage," perhaps we would all do well to pay more attention to *which* usage seems appropriate *when* and under *what* circumstances. Rather than seeking to fix a set of rules to govern how people should speak and write, we might best maintain an openness to change.

Yes, of course. There are no *rules* controlling how a language is used; there are only "habits."

There are no rules, but there *are* habits!

The writer who desires to communicate simple information clearly and quickly has to know what are likely to be the habits of his or her readers. In order to allow readers to attend directly to *what* they are saying, rather than to their peculiar *way* of saying it, journalists (essayists, writers of textbooks, et al.) must adapt their own personal language to the language the majority of their audience is accustomed to. That is the discipline of learning to write in order to communicate information efficiently.

In other words, the "situation" to which the informational writer's language must be "appropriate" is rather well defined at any one time. It is true that the public's language habits are in a constant process of change; but most obvious changes are relatively superficial, involving vocabulary rather than sentence structure, for instance. (Many notable changes in language habits are also themselves fleeting or related to a narrow subculture rather than to what we think of as The General Public.)

Within this system of the writer's desire to communicate information efficiently and the public's identifiable, basic language habits, it is possible to formulate several general standards for effective writing. In these circumstances, which are not universal but are quite real and even necessary, some uses of language and other meaningful visual signs are "correct," and others are "flaws."

The basic standards are relatively few, and they are all grounded squarely in the writer's pragmatic need to communicate information to the general public.

How to Rank Writing Flaws

Since we have a clearly defined goal—to communicate information—we can even rank the basic errors actually encountered today from "worst" to "least serious."

The worst flaws would be those that prevent communication absolutely, and the least serious would be those that make communication somewhat less efficient than the more customary usage would do. At the bottom of the list would be those usages, of vocabulary or even punctuation, which seem purely matters of convention, determined only by habit and very little by the need to communicate information.

The general recommendations about "correctness" and "effectiveness" that I shall offer in what follows do not cover all conceivable cases. Just as a viable, living language is (by definition) capable of dealing with infinite possibilities within human experience, so are there infinite ways of "going wrong" with respect to customary language habits. I am assuming that the most elementary features of American English are already familiar to all readers of this book; I am not attempting to teach the language per se. Rather, I am offering some suggestions about writing that language, as opposed to thinking and speaking it, and in particular about writing it in such a way that it communicates information effectively.

Out of all conceivable writing flaws, I have selected those that are most common today. We will deal with them more or less in order of the degree to which each type of error acts to prevent communication of information.

YOUR GENERAL GOALS

What every writer must do to improve his or her ability to communicate effectively is, first, to develop the general ability to see her or his writing as it will look to others on the page; and second, to learn to beware of his or her own customary weaknesses as a communicative writer.

Everyone has certain habits that are his or her own, as distinct from any other person's and from those of the impersonal general public. To communicate effectively, our writing must conform to the general habits. That means that each of us needs to become conscious of how our habits differ from the most common ones and to learn how to modify ours. (We must so conform at least when we are writing primarily in order to communicate information; at other times, of course, we must be ourselves.)

Learning to write effectively, therefore, is very largely a process of gathering certain conscious standards that need to be applied again and again to one's own writing. You may have no trouble at all with misplaced modifiers, for instance, though we all should know that such trouble is possible. But you may discover that you are constantly tempted to use pronouns whose reference is not clear. Both this section and Part 3 are designed to help you identify your own problems and to help you deal with those problems once you have identified them.

Problem I: Making Sense

First and most important of all, of course, your writing must *make sense.* You could not hope to communicate at all if the visual signs you put on the page seemed meaningless nonsense to your reader.

Vkfxg hljf sfkgkng mjxg mz,d xdnxd

A cryptographer would have no trouble at all discovering that this strange assemblage of signs is part of my first sentence above, typed on the wrong line. But your reader is not a cryptographer! Included as part of this necessity for the communicative writer to make sense are all matters having to do with logic, even probability; coherence or organization of the essay or news story; and reasoning. Much of a journalist's job in this respect is often taken care of by relatively standard patterns of organization (the "inverted pyramid," for instance). But even the simple news story cannot make sense if the chronology of a sequence of events is not lucidly presented, to cite only one way even a simple story may go wrong.

All the most elementary language habits we can expect native speakers to be accustomed to also appear under this heading. The following sentence, for example, literally does not make sense:

Mary writes easier than Bill.

A reader can figure out the intended meaning of the sentence without difficulty, no doubt; but he should not be forced to "figure" at all. The words *writes* and *easier* do not go together to "make sense" in our language. Every such fundamental betrayal of the expected language patterns takes the risk of being mere nonsense.

A verb with no subject, a singular subject with a plural verb (or vice versa), or an apparently uncaused change in verb tense is also likely to seem nonsensical. Reading one's own writing aloud and attending to the visual aspect of writing should be sufficient for most writers to eliminate almost all of these elementary errors.

PROBLEM II: PRONOUNS

As we have seen in Chapter II, pronouns are often a basic means by which words are bound together in order to communicate meaning. Problems in agreement between a pronoun and the word or phrase it is supposed to refer to, in a pronoun's clarity or precision of reference, or in a pronoun's having no word or phrase to refer to are likely to create serious difficulties in communication:

Mary and Sue gave Tom a piece of <u>her</u> mind.
(*Whose mind?* we might ask.)

Since the doorbell was ringing, <u>it</u> meant that someone was outside.
(What precisely is the meaning of *it* in this sentence?)

Many young writers seem to have trouble making significant use of pronouns these days; perhaps this has always been a problem.

Pronoun difficulty can pose as serious a threat to communication in writing as elementary failure to make sense. Fortunately, most writers can isolate particular occasions when they are likely to use a pronoun inadequately and can thus learn to deal with the potential problem fairly readily. At the very least, writers who characteristically have "pronoun trouble" can rather easily read over their writing one time looking for every single pronoun they have used and checking the agreement, clarity, and precision of each.

PROBLEM III: SENTENCES

The sentence is the basic unit of meaning in writing. Grouping words in certain ways that make sense is the basic task of the communicative writer. As we have already seen, the visual means of grouping words and phrases into meaningful sentences involves what may be considered the "translation" of spoken stresses and pauses into visual signs. Punctuation, in other words, has a lot to do with the simple communication of meaning, since punctuation often controls the grouping of written or printed words and phrases into sentences.

The most frequent errors of this sort that we find today, as one might expect, have to do with a writer's making it seem on the visible page that some words are linked to others with which, in fact, they do not make sense:

You may be interested to know, on the other hand, you may not.

A reader would ordinarily expect the object of *to know* to follow *on the other hand* in this sentence, as in the following example:

You may be interested to know, on the other hand, that you have made a serious error in punctuation.

The commas in the first example, in other words, do not adequately separate the second half of this compound sentence from the first half.

The opposite problem—separating words that in fact "belong" together—is equally common:

My father hit me. Which is hard to take.

These are not really two separate sentences (thoughts); they should not be separated by the period. In the context of other sentences coming before and after, the separation would be especially confusing.

All problems with sentence fragments, with so-called run-on's, and with other kinds of compound sentence fall into this category. The least serious of the errors in major punctuation of this type are mainly matters of convention; but the most serious can prevent communication altogether:

There was no one home but I waited anyway.

Leaving out the customary comma after *home* is not too serious in this sentence, but without it the reader could expect something like "There was no one home but me." Not finding what she or he expects may confuse a reader.

> Jean-Paul Marat actually thought of himself as being the Revolution. The Revolution that must kill thousands because of Marat's so-called love of the French people.

This, on the other hand, is a serious error. No reader could know that the words *The Revolution* following the first period do not begin a new sentence whose verb will come after the clause between *that* and *people*. Since no verb for *The Revolution* does follow the clause, the passage simply does not make sense. Imagine trying to read it aloud. The period in the middle would make you drop your voice and take a breath. Where would you be at the "end"?

Some writers do find it difficult to get used to the customary ways of showing in writing or printing how words and phrases are grouped into sentences, separated from the words and phrases in other sentences. It seems to me that once a writer understands the *meaning* of the relevant punctuation marks, by considering the relations between speaking and writing, she or he can make rapid progress.

PROBLEM IV: MODIFIERS

Placement of words carries a great deal of meaning in American English. In speech we sometimes connect words and phrases with others by stress, intonation, clever use of pauses, and so on. In print or writing, however, simple placement is almost all the writer has at his disposal. Forgetting this may result in embarrassing confusion:

> Hanging from the banyan tree, Miss Prim saw the baboon. (What was the *baboon* doing while Miss Prim was swinging around in the tree?)

Once alerted to the possibility of such confusions, most writers can eliminate misplaced modifiers without too much difficulty.

OTHER PROBLEMS

Each of the following four chapters treats in somewhat more detail the errors young writers most commonly make by failing to make sense, using pronouns imprecisely or misleadingly, improperly grouping words into sentences, and misplacing modifiers. The final chapter in this section mentions several miscellaneous errors that also appear frequently in student writing today but that seem to me somewhat less significant.

Placing the section on Effectiveness in Part 3 *after* this section on Correctness may in itself be misleading. Often, it seems, what starts out as a basic inadequacy in *style*—wordiness, imprecise diction, inactive verbs and "overactive" nouns, or simply awkwardness—ends up as an elementary error in grammar or punctuation. When the style is made more effective—more precise, dynamic, and straightforward—the elementary error either disappears or is left so obvious that it cannot be missed. In practice, Effectiveness and Correctness cannot be separated.

As you read the following chapters, bear in mind that you may not often be tempted, if ever, to make every one of the errors discussed. You may make others, in fact, that are not treated at all. Even if a few of your own characteristic writing "flaws" are not as basic or significant as the ones dealt with, they may still be departures from customary usage that you will want to know how to correct. With respect to the finer points of word choice and punctuation, customs vary from audience to audience and from publication to publication. Most particular "situations"—publishers, magazines or newspapers, even English teachers—have Style Manuals or Handbooks to define precisely those conventions "appropriate" in each specific case.

But such so-called finer points are not our first concern. In all instances, the writer's primary job must be to make certain that his or her writing communicates information clearly and quickly. All of the general recommendations about style in Part 3 on Effectiveness are designed to help you make your writing accomplish this essential task. Likewise, all of the customary language habits discussed in Part 2 as standards of Correctness are those that may most directly affect your ability to communicate information in writing.

Chapter V

MAKING SENSE

What teachers, school administrators, parents, and employers evidently find most shocking about the writing of many young people finishing high school today is the fact that it often contains what seem the most elementary of "errors": language usages that do not correspond to conventional patterns. The problem does not seem to be that these uses correspond to new patterns, but that they do not correspond to any pattern at all and thus simply do not "make sense." Other usages may correspond to patterns encountered in one contemporary subculture or another, and in the "situation" may be quite "appropriate," but do not conform to what are clearly understood as more generally "appropriate" patterns.

Just as it is important not to be disturbed by the necessity to conform to impersonal social modes in order to communicate effectively, let us remind ourselves that it is equally necessary to avoid overly emotional responses to nonconventional language patterns. But they should be recognized as such and brought under conscious control.

The Problem

The fact remains that such a sentence as we observed in the last chapter—

Mary writes easier than Bill

—does not correspond to generally accepted patterns of language and thus could not be said to communicate effectively. Perhaps in some less broadly inclusive social situation, this sentence might

59

seem quite conventional, the words *easier* and *writes* quite normally "going together" to make sense; but such is not the widest usage.

The following slightly different sentence, which is what actually appeared in a recent student essay, does not conventionally appear in any written language:

Mary writes easer then Bill.

No one knowingly says, thinks, or writes *easer* in such a "situation." Yet this sort of thing is what one finds more and more often in student writing today.

These two errors are comparably elementary. Once the writer's essential task has been clearly defined and understood—to communicate information clearly and rapidly, through a visual, verbal medium, to the widest possible audience—the difference between what seems "a grammatical error" and what may have been "a typing error" tends to disappear. Neither usage communicates effectively; both must be eliminated.

Generally "How-To"

Keeping in mind at all times your essential task and striving at all times to *see* your writing on the page as it will look to a reader who does not know you seem to me the best ways to start eliminating such errors from your writing.

Students who have special difficulty distinguishing language usages that are suitable to their own most common personal circumstances from those most common to the general public can make rapid progress by reading attentively, perhaps aloud, communicative writing aimed at that public, developing a feel for the "public language" as distinguished from their own "personal language." Since the public language does surround all of us, in one way or another, developing such a sense should not be too difficult for anyone who decides it is genuinely worth doing.

The hardest problem in eliminating truly elementary errors that prevent one's writing from making sense is that the errors tend to come in bunches. One of your sentences may seem wrong. You know what you mean and why you chose those particular words and phrases in the first place, but your "ear" tells you that the pattern is possibly unconventional or just wrong. But, try as you may, you cannot put your finger precisely on the basic problem.

Such an instance will often include not one but several related errors, not only of "correctness" but also of style. Your hardest problem will be to sort out the various kinds of difficulty you have unfortunately encountered so that you can go about communicating the information that you need to convey.

One suggestion the organization of this book makes to a writer in such a predicament is to use the "hierarchy of writing flaws." Don't simply stare at the suspicious sentence, looking for all possible errors at once. Check out each of the various possibilities, one at a time, in order of the most to the least serious threat to communication. The errors treated in this chapter are those that you should be able to spot the most quickly and eliminate the most easily.

BASIC PATTERNS

If your writing does not conform to the basic patterns by which American English usually comes to "make sense," obviously it will fail to communicate.

Any native speaker is familiar with the most elementary patterns and can usually recognize them, or their absence, even in his or her own writing. Of course the possibilities for going wrong in this respect are still, as always, infinite. Anything can happen, especially in a quickly written first draft. But on cool consideration, most writers might be expected to spot such inadequacies as this:

> When her husband would come home from work, the 19th-century wife would probably be mending some clothes, by hand, or just too tired to cater to the needs of her provider.

Possibly, once again, this represents an inadequate "translation" of speech to writing. In any case it seems clear that the intention was to make *would be* function as the first part of two different predicates: *"would be* mending" and *"would be* too tired." The essential problem with that intention, which might conceivably be brought off in speech, is that these two phrases are grammatically quite different. *Would be mending* is in fact virtually one single "word" (a verb); whereas *would be tired* is two "words," *would-be* (a verb) and *tired* (an adjective). The same construction, *would be,* just cannot function simultaneously in two such different ways.

I am not certain anyone else would describe this problem exactly as I have, but we can be relatively sure that most readers trying to spot the difficulty in this example would focus upon the last part of the sentence, and especially upon *or just too tired.* Something necessary for making sense seems left out. Indeed, it is: *would be* has to be repeated for the whole to perform that most basic function of making sense:

> When her husband would come home from work, the 19th-century wife would probably be mending some clothes, by hand, or would be just too tired to cater to the needs of her provider.

Whatever we may say about the importance, the accuracy or truth, and the economy and precision of expression in this sentence with the *would be* phrase repeated, it at least can be said to communicate adequately a general thought.

The departure from the basic patterns that appears most often in student writing these days is not so clearly a simple oversight as the one above. No doubt our conversation is beginning to employ adjectives, words that usually modify nouns, interchangeably with adverbs, words that usually modify verbs, as in that sentence about Mary and Bill. This still looks like a fundamental error in informational writing, however, and it will still threaten communication.

You may recognize this sentence, slightly tidied up, from a previous example:

> If all members of the low-income family do not <u>pull together real tight,</u> the family can easily fall to pieces because of its unstable financial status.

I hope the underlined words, "pull together real tight," stand out as unconventional to anyone reading this sentence carefully. Something basic is wrong.

Alerted to the differences that may distinguish spoken, popular conversation from informational writing, you should notice that this is a verb phrase, the active part of that first section of the sentence. You should therefore suspect that the problem is created by a word, which in writing should be reserved for use with nouns and similar constructions, being used instead as a part of the verb phrase. Yes, *tight* is the problem here.

The student who wrote this sentence may have been remembering the conventional phrase "to pull [something] tight." But that is clearly not the meaning in this sentence: the family is not going to be "pulled tight"; on the contrary, the family is itself doing the "pulling." The student intends to say something about the *manner* of "pulling." For this, an adverb—one of those words that fairly often end in *-ly* in English—is required.

But if we simply say *tightly* instead of *tight,* the conventional pattern may indeed appear—

[Family members] pull together real tightly . . .

—but the problem of making sense still remains. We do not usually employ the word *tightly* to describe how someone "pulls" something; together these two words do not communicate anything. An adverbial construction is indeed needed, but not that particular one. Perhaps simply *hard?* We do often say "to pull hard" and may even say "to pull hard together." Try it:

If all members of the low-income family do not pull together real hard, the family can easily fall to pieces because of its unstable financial status.

That may not be elegant prose destined for a Pulitzer Prize, but it does seem to get the job done. At least it is an improvement.

The point to remember is that, when a verb phrase seems wrong to you, check first to see if the problem arises, most basically, because you have used an adjective where an adverb would fit more conventionally.

Other, less predictable difficulties may occur in even these basic patterns. You will have to rely on your "ear" and your understanding of how to translate speech to writing, as well of course as on advice from an editor or a teacher, to help you spot and correct these elementary errors.

SUBJECTS AND VERBS

The two most fundamental elements in the basic unit of meaning, the sentence, are the subject and the verb. Problems in conventionally coordinating these two elements threaten the meaningfulness of a sentence as fast as any other type of problem.

Probably students have always had difficulty making subjects and verbs go together in form precisely as in the meaning they intend to communicate. This seems to be the second most common elementary error young writers make today.

Consider the following sentence, which appeared originally in a discussion of communicative devices other than language:

A tear or a smile are nice but may be misunderstood.

When the young woman who wrote this sentence was told it included an elementary error, she looked at it a moment, seemed to be mentally pronouncing it to herself (an excellent strategy), and then, saying "Oh, yes!," made the following correction:

A tear or smile are nice but may be misunderstood.

Eliminating the *a* before *smile* does make the problem less striking, but the problem itself remains.

The first version in fact provides a better clue to the basic error than the second. Each of the possible subjects of the verb in this sentence is singular, but the verb itself is plural. Such a disparity does not make sense.

A tear or [a] smile <u>is</u> nice but may be misunderstood.

This revision makes the subject and the verb "agree" in number; both are now singular.

"Disagreement" or lack of "agreement" between subject and verb is a serious error that always prevents precise and efficient communication.

Such a problem almost always appears when the subject of the sentence is rather long:

Education in high school and the lower grades are not sufficient preparation for living.

Sex and violence, according to New York's most famous film critic, is the theme of the typical American movie today.

In both of these sentences, the verb is different in number from the subject. In both cases a noun which is not the subject of the sentence but which does appear close to the verb has evidently influenced the writer's choice of verb form. The first writer thought, *"Grades are* not sufficient," and the second writer thought, "The *theme is* . . ."

In the first sentence, in fact, *Education,* even though it does not appear right next to the verb, is (both in meaning and in form) the subject of the sentence.

> Education in high school and the lower grades <u>is</u> not sufficient preparation for living.

In the second sentence, the question is slightly more complex. It is barely possible that the words "sex and violence" are used together so often in a discussion like this one that they have come to represent a single concept. This phrase may seem like a single "word," *sex-and-violence,* rather than two separate words linked by *and.* The sentence, as written, just might communicate normally.

When in doubt, however, the informational writer should be conservative in grammar; his or her goal depends upon matching the language habits of the greatest number of readers. Really basic habits—such as agreement in number between subject and verb—are not likely to change. When faced with a choice between a normal, *basic* habit and a relatively new habit involving only words or phrases, the informational writer should probably choose to conform to the basic pattern:

> Sex and violence, according to New York's most famous film critic, are the theme of the typical American movie today.

Printed this way, the construction *are the theme* may "sound" funny. If so, something should probably be changed. We have already seen, however, that *is* instead of *are* will not do; some other change might be tried:

> Sex and violence . . . <u>are</u> the twin <u>themes</u> . . .

or perhaps—

Sex and violence . . . <u>constitute</u> the main theme . . .

Bear in mind that the noun following the verb does not normally affect the verb's number in American English (as it does, for example, in Latin). If it sounds funny, however, don't use it. The following revision may be the safest:

> Sex and violence, according to New York's most famous film critic, are the twin themes of the typical American movie today.

If you do discover that you sometimes, or even often, have difficulty matching subjects and verbs, you should develop the habit of reading over your first draft looking for every instance in which you have a relatively long phrase functioning as the subject of a sentence. In news stories this is very common, especially in "lead" sentences. "Long subjects" are likely to be either compound subjects (two or three nouns linked by *and,* making a plural, or by *or,* making a singular) or noun phrases in which the subject is separated from the verb by a preposition such as *of, to, in,* or *by* and several related words. (Incidentally, if you are ever uncertain about which form of a verb is singular and which is plural, just say each form out loud with a singular pronoun ["it, she, or he (<u>verb</u>)s"] and then with a plural pronoun ["they or we (<u>verb</u>)"].)

Locating every potential trouble spot is half the battle. What do you do then?

One student of mine suggested that it might be smart to eliminate all long subjects. That would probably be inconvenient for many of us, however, although it would simplify the task of matching subjects and verbs, since the problem is indeed most likely to be created by a separation of the two either by a prepositional phrase or by the subject's being itself compound rather than simple. No, such constructions are necessary. Instead of eliminating them, we should *find* them and simply make sure that the verb agrees in number with the subject. If the first simple revision then sounds strange, further revision may be necessary, as we have seen.

> A newspaper's popularity and success depends a great deal upon the language the newspaper uses.

Tsk, tsk.

TENSE

Last fall, a student asked me, "How do I make my writing less tense?"

The comment on his paper that had led to the question referred instead, of course, to the tense of his verb in one sentence. Relations in time among various events are extremely significant in many news stories, and these relations are most clearly indicated by the tense—past or pluperfect (the *had* form of a verb), present or future—of the writer's verbs. It is important to use those tenses that accurately indicate the temporal relations among the events being described.

Imprecision in this regard poses a serious threat to communication. Consider this sentence, for example, written some time ago by one of my students:

The teeth <u>will last</u> only so long, so after a person is chewing for many years the teeth <u>start to develop</u> small holes in them.

The temporal relations that these verb tenses imply are not probable, to say the least. The first verb, *will last,* may be fine, if the writer does intend to refer to the future. But in the last half of the sentence, the first event referred to—the chewing—has to occur *before* the second event—the cavities' developing. Having both events referred to by verbs in the same tense simply does not make sense. The correct formulation would probably read as follows:

The teeth will last only so long, so after a person has been chewing for many years the teeth start to develop small holes in them.

Fortunately, most writers have no difficulty handling various tenses. It seems self-evident *which* one to use *when.*

There is only one exception, the pluperfect. When you are recounting a series of events in the past and it is necessary to refer to another event from still earlier, the *had* form of the verb is absolutely necessary.

The most significant step for a writer who has trouble with tenses is simply to discover that he does. Once on the lookout, most writers can not only spot troublesome sentences but also resolve the difficulty in them. You can see immediately that the thinking represented in the following sentence is fuzzy once you have learned to scrutinize it closely:

A battle had been fought, and I won.

I think that sentence, considered carefully, would sound funny to most of us. The problem is that these two events, a battle being fought and "I" winning, must have occurred in the same general time frame. Anything else does not make sense. But the tense of the two verbs is different. To make sense, both verbs must be either past or pluperfect. In this case, one may assume that the first verb corresponds more closely to the intended meaning—

A battle had been fought, and I <u>had</u> won

—although the other possibility would be equally correct:

A battle <u>was</u> fought, and I won.

One or the other revision must be made. Only the writer can know which alternative he meant.

Here is one more example:

I went to the airport to pick Maria up, but when I got there Maria's mother and Debbie's father were already waiting. Debbie went to California with Maria.

Even assuming that there is a good reason for delaying this final sentence so long, its verb still does not make sense. The time of Debbie's "going to California" must be prior to the time of the other events recounted here. That difference in the time frame of the event must be shown in the verb's tense.

In order to make sense, the last sentence must read, "Debbie had gone . . ."

NORMAL USAGE

Almost everyone's personal language differs from what I have been calling the public language in, for one thing, the unique way each of us *combines* certain words. In "normal usage" many combinations of words are so usual that any variation from custom when employing them turns out to be confusing and incommunicative.

We have seen one example of such an idiosyncratic variation from the norm, saying "to pull together *tightly*" rather than the usual "to pull together *hard*." Even such a simple change from the customary phrasing can prevent clear and rapid communication of information.

Consider this sentence, for example, taken from a recent student essay which was in form rather like an "editorial":

One may look into this event a message for all.

According to conventional usage, a person does not *look* something *into* something else. The words cannot function meaningfully that way. A person either *looks* in a certain manner ("he looked away quickly") or "looks *like*" something or someone else, or "looks *for*" or "*at*" something. You can even "look *in* someone's eyes" or "look *into* the wild blue yonder"; but you cannot have someone *look* something *into* something else.

The intended meaning here might be—

One may <u>look into</u> this event and <u>find</u> a message for all

—or perhaps:

One may <u>see</u> in this event a message for all.

From time to time every writer discovers that a combination of several words that he or she is accustomed to employing— often a verb and a preposition—is not "normal usage." If the writer's main goal is to communicate information efficiently without calling attention to his or her manner of writing, it is the writer's habit that must be changed.

Not long ago, I saw a student essay recounting the evolution of an English word's meanings, a peculiarly difficult subject to write about without having trouble with ordinary usage. The following sentence seemed particularly problematic:

Generating from the meanings of the word *prone* from the 15th century to the present is significant in that <u>its meanings are still used</u> and will continue to be a part of our language.

(I have quietly converted the student's word *it's* to the correct, possessive form here.)

The thought is quite hard to follow in this sentence, isn't it? Let us examine why that is so. I think we might say there are two basic problem areas, the first appearing in the section *is significant in that.* The style here is certainly ineffective, and we will later learn (in Part 3) how to avoid such awkward constructions as *in that.* . . . But we have an even more basic error here too: what is the subject of the verb *is?* You might expect it to be the word *generating* which begins the sentence, although when we start reading the sentence for the first time it does not seem this will be true. And even looking back, it does not seem probable that the writer could have meant that "generating" something "is significant." In fact, *what* is being "generated"? No, actually no noun or noun phrase appears in the first part of this sentence that can meaningfully function as the subject of the predicate *is significant.* Just *what* is significant?

It is only a guess, but perhaps the intended meaning was as follows:

> The meanings of the word *prone* generated from the 15th century to the present are significant . . .

(I am not certain that we normally say that "meanings" are "generated," but perhaps in context this might be all right.)

The section of the sentence I am even more interested in is the underlined part: *its meanings are still used.* I hope this construction seems odd to everyone. The fact is, we do not "use meanings." This combination of words will not do. We use *words.* Words *have* meanings. "Meanings are used" is not a conventional way to speak or write our language.

Since everyone may occasionally employ a combination of words—verb and preposition, or as in the second example, verb and object or complement—it may seem peculiarly difficult to spot variations from "normal usage" in your own writing. A young writer who has persistent difficulty in this regard needs more experience reading examples of "public language." Practice in reading newspapers, magazine articles, nonfiction books, and so on may be the answer. Reading them aloud may help train your ear to hear the conventional combinations.

For the record, the following revision of the sentence about *prone* seems to my own ear a considerable improvement:

The meanings of the word *prone* generated from the 15th century to the present are [especially] significant because all of them are still part of our language.

"Logic"

For lack of a better term (which is equally easy to write), I rather often scrawl the word *logic* in the margin of student essays. A writer has to be careful that the thinking embodied in the words he places on the page is reasonable and precise. Once alerted to the possibility of going astray in this regard, most students have little difficulty avoiding errors. But it is important to be sure your writing always "makes sense" in this way also.

Here is a sentence that does not:

At present woman is still combatting the inferiority man has always associated with her sex.

Let us suppose that you discovered that sentence in a feature article or an editorial of your own. Scrutinized very carefully (as all your sentences should be), it may strike you as odd. What do you do about it?

First you might look for an adjective hiding in the verb phrase (no, not there), and then quickly check the main elements, subject and verb, to see if the problem lies in lack of agreement. *Woman is still combatting . . . :* no problem there. The tenses coordinate precisely with the time relation of the events referred to, and the fundamental word combinations seem conventional: someone *is combatting* something, and someone *has always associated* something *with* something else. Fine.

But there is still a peculiar feeling about this sentence. Perhaps it is the vague abstractions "woman" and "man," although it may seem more basic than that. Look at it again:

At present woman is still combatting the inferiority man has always associated with her sex.

"Woman is combatting" *what?* You see, it does not exactly make sense to say that "woman" is fighting or resisting or "combatting" *inferiority.* In fact, the writer of this sentence seems to believe that women are *not* inferior; the inferiority men have always associated with the opposite sex, she feels, is not real.

The thinking represented by the sentence is fuzzy, imprecise, confused.

A considerable revision is probably necessary to set things right. Does this seem to straighten out the original thought?

> At present woman is still combatting the mistaken notion man has always maintained that persons of her sex are inferior.

All of us writers have to be tough on ourselves. We must make a consistent effort to be certain that our sentences *say* precisely what we *mean*, word by word, and phrase by phrase. This is not a "fine point" about "polishing up your style." It is a basic principle necessary for making sense.

ERRORS BUNCHED UP

All too often for a writer's peace of mind, errors and stylistic weaknesses come all clustered together. When an idea is peculiarly complex or not particularly well thought out, the sentence we write may often seem wrong in some strange way, and it may turn out that there is not one single problem with it but several all run together.

The following sentence is not overly complicated, though it is wrong, and it includes more than one basic error:

> When something once thought to be true is proven false, would mean that it was never true in the beginning.

Look at this sentence closely; if necessary, read it slowly aloud. Yes, one basic difficulty is obvious: the verb *would mean* has no subject. Perhaps a word has been left out? Try adding *it?*

> When something once thought to be true is proven false, <u>it would mean</u> that it was never true in the beginning.

That seems to make bad matters worse. There are two *it*'s now, each referring to a different thing. And what does the new *it* refer to in the first place? (We will see other examples of this sort of basic difficulty with pronouns in the next chapter.)

It is important to spot the verb with no subject immediately and to try to remedy that situation as simply as possible. But in this case, something else is clearly wrong, too. Consider the thought that the writer apparently is trying to communicate. I believe that the "logic" is obscure. The thought is not precisely a matter of *when* at all, not concerned with how things are related in time; nor is it a matter of *meaning,* as the apparently essential words *would mean* seem to imply. Those ideas are not in fact essential to the thought, and the words suggesting those ideas should be eliminated.

Try another word instead of *when;* perhaps *if:*

> If something once thought to be true is proven false . . . it was never true in the beginning.

That does seem an improvement. Maybe we do not need anything where I have left the blank [. . .] except a simple comma to indicate a brief pause.

Still, you may suspect that the writer wanted to stress something about *how we know* when a belief or opinion is in fact false. This might require a word or two in the blank.

> If something once thought to be true is proven false, we may assume that it was never true in the beginning.

Whether or not the writer would agree that this version actually communicates his or her intended meaning, perhaps the general point is clear: even basic errors sometimes come mixed together, and correcting one may reveal another that needs correcting also.

Unfortunately, an even more typical example of difficulties that come together is the following sentence:

> Three ways by which the newspaper influences and enlightens its readers is through editorials, columns, and editorial cartoons.

It may seem that the most basic error in this sentence is the fact that the subject *ways* and the verb *is* do not agree in number. That is certainly true, and it is a typical example of disagreement, with a prepositional phrase separating subject and verb.

Notice, however, that simply correcting this problem does not make the sentence altogether correct:

> Three ways by which the newspaper influences and enlightens its readers are through editorials, columns, and editorial cartoons.

That may even "sound" worse.

The basic pattern according to which thoughts are related to each other in this sentence does not make sense:

. . . ways by which . . . are through . . .

This "structural" problem may be even more basic than the problem of agreement between subject and verb. Without resolving the problem in the basic pattern, the writer of this sentence could not hope to communicate the information precisely and effectively.

If you should find a sentence like this one, this "fouled up," in your own writing, you may know that it is wrong somehow but not know how to go about revising it. When that happens, you should scratch the sentence out entirely, rethink the passage in which it appears as a whole, and write a totally new sentence to communicate the information the sentence should convey. Never hesitate to rewrite a sentence totally.

In this case, once you recognize that the most basic trouble lies in the pattern represented by the words *ways . . . are through,* a simple change may immediately come to mind:

Three ways by which the newspaper influences and enlightens its readers <u>are</u> editorials, columns, and editorial cartoons.

The *ways* simply *are* such and such; they are not *through* anything. Of course, if you chose to rewrite the whole sentence, changing the emphasis, you might write simply—

The newspaper influences and enlightens its readers through editorials, columns, and editorial cartoons.

The main thing to recognize is that *ways by which* and *through* cannot both appear, related as they were originally in this sentence.

Avoiding Basic Errors in Making Sense

Even most inexperienced writers have little difficulty making sense most of the time, especially if they are accustomed to seeing their writing on the page as it will appear to others. No one consistently makes all the types of elementary error discussed in this chapter: in basic patterns, agreement between subject and verb, verb tense, normal usage, and "logic."

But many of us may discover that we tend to make one or even two types of error persistently. When we have recognized that characteristic weakness in our writing, it should be fairly easy to devise a strategy for dealing with it.

If you often make *mistakes in "grammar,"* or the most basic patterns by which a language use comes to make sense, then try reading your writing slowly aloud, trying to sound just like the typical writer of the conventional, "establishment" publication you are most familiar with. (Familiarize yourself with several.) You might especially check your verb phrases to see if you have used an adjective where an adverb would be more normal.

If you often make *mistakes in agreement* between subject and verb, learn to recognize these essential elements and check to see whether or not they agree before passing your writing on to someone else. You may find it helpful in particular to look for sentences in which the subject is either compound or phrased so that a prepositional construction intervenes between the subject and the verb.

If you often make *mistakes in the tenses* of your verbs, try thinking carefully about each verb and how the event it refers to relates in time to the other events you are writing about. In particular, make sure you have used the *had* form to refer to every event still farther in the past than the other events in the past you are talking about.

If you often combine words in ways that are not what others recognize as *normal usage,* you also might find it useful to read your writing slowly aloud, pretending to be writing for the most conventional magazine or newspaper you are familiar with. Pay particular attention to the second sections of your sentences, to the words that come after the verbs.

And if you often write sentences whose *"logic" seems imprecise* or askew, read every sentence you write very thoughtfully, taking especial care to make sure you have perfectly matched your precise meaning by the words you have written down.

Remember that most of your basic language habits are probably quite conventional without your making any special effort. Only one or two of them may need some extra attention.

Chapter VI

PRONOUNS

Again and again we may observe that words come to communicate meaning by the precise ways they are linked together. As a result, the most elementary problems the writer may encounter, those errors we explored in the last chapter, all have to do with just how words are linked together in American English in order to "make sense." Likewise, the next chapter is concerned with the ways the writer links words and phrases written or printed on the visual page into sentences that communicate information.

Pronouns also serve to *link together* thoughts verbally expressed. Consider again these opening sentences from Twain's *Life on the Mississippi:*

> The Mississippi is well worth reading about. It is not a commonplace river, but on the contrary is in all ways remarkable.

The thought about not being "commonplace" is efficiently linked to the thought "the Mississippi" by means of that simple pronoun *it*. This is such an ordinary communicative device that we may not even notice it. Everybody knows how to use and how to understand such a simple pronoun.

Almost every writer, on the other hand, encounters situations now and then in which the use of a pronoun does not seem so clear and easy. Since pronouns are such a fundamental device for linking thoughts together, any fuzziness in their usage will threaten communication immediately. Perhaps it is worth while to consider, right away, what even such a simple pronoun as Twain's *it* accomplishes.

Pronouns have three essential functions. First, of course, a pronoun does not have much meaning all by itself; it gains meaning in speech or writing by referring to something else, usually a

76

noun that has been written or spoken sometime before. The pronoun *it* in the Twain sentences refers back to an "antecedent," the words *The Mississippi,* for its meaning.

Second, in order to refer a reader's attention clearly and quickly back to that preceding phrase, the pronoun must agree with its antecedent in number and gender: that merely means that *The Mississippi* is a single thing, instead of being more than one thing and instead of being a person. Every native speaker of the language knows that only a few pronouns can be used to refer to "a single thing": *it, this, that,* and possibly one or two others. The speaker or writer would probably choose between these several alternatives without thinking much about it, depending on the emphasis and so on that he wanted to communicate. The most important thing necessary for the pronoun to accomplish its "linking" task is for it to be the same in number and gender as the word or words it refers to.

And finally, if the pronoun is to accomplish this task its reference must be immediately clear; you cannot have several possible thoughts, all different, to which the pronoun might be referring. In the Twain sentence, no other "single thing" is mentioned at all before the pronoun *it* appears. The reader knows immediately, without even thinking, that the sentence that begins with *it* is talking about *the Mississippi.*

RELATED ERRORS

If we are not careful, we may sometimes confuse or mislead our readers by using pronouns that fail to perform one or another of these three essential functions. Consider this passage from an essay on Fitzgerald's *The Great Gatsby:*

> Gatsby and Nick Carraway live in West Egg; Daisy and Tom Buchanon live in East Egg. Since the two villages are separated by water, <u>it</u> signifies that there is a barrier between Daisy and Gatsby that can never be overcome.

The general idea is communicated fairly well, and it seems an interesting and original perception. But consider just how precisely the words, one by one, communicate the writer's intended meaning.

What, for example, does that little *it* mean? Just *what* is doing the "signifying" here?

Well, we might say that it is the fact itself that two characters live in one place and two others live in another place which "signifies" what the writer suggests. Yes, but that seems too much for that little *it* to refer to. That is not "a single thing" like Twain's *Mississippi;* it is much more complex than that.

The error would seem to be that the pronoun *it* has no antecedent at all. It does not refer back to one word or a simple phrase for its meaning. Thus, it has no meaning unless we work at it.

Here is another example of what may seem the same error:

Through the proper use of language, human relationships become closer. It presents an easier way of communicating.

A moment's thought will probably reveal that the writer's intention is to have *it* refer back to the word *language.* In his or her thinking, the meaning of *it* is quite clear. Unfortunately that meaning is not clear on the page.

The nearest noun, in fact, which the reader remembers best when he comes to *it,* is "human relationships." That will not do at all, of course, since it is plural and *it* is not. The other most memorable word from what precedes the pronoun is not *language* but "the proper *use*" since that is where the main stress of the first sentence falls. Faced with this confusion, the reader will be at a loss simply to understand that word *it.*

In such a situation, either considerable revision is called for (in case the emphasis of the first sentence is not what the writer intended), or the noun the writer is thinking of should itself be used instead of a pronoun:

Through the proper use of language, human relationships become closer. Language presents an easier way of communicating.

That change alone makes this passage communicate much more effectively, which is after all the most important thing. (Later we might ask further, "easier than *what?*")

MORE AGREEMENT

Since the writer usually does know what he or she wants to say, and thus knows the meaning the pronouns should communicate to the reader, he or she may sometimes be tempted to use one which—to someone else—will seem to have no meaning, to refer back to no antecedent.

Some writers also have a tendency to pause, thinking about what they are going to say, between sentences that eventually turn out to be closely related. As a result, a singular might change to a plural in the writer's thinking without any reason for the shift appearing on the written page. This would be confusing, as in the following example:

> To any man entered in a National Sailfish Regatta, a woman is a disastrous obstacle. They are forever getting in a man's way.

This was in fact the first sentence in a student essay. Notice that there is no noun to which *They* in the second sentence could refer. All the nouns preceding the pronoun are singular.

Clearly the young woman who wrote this sentence intended to refer to *a woman,* which in her thinking represented a plural; or perhaps she had slightly changed her thinking by the time she began writing the second sentence. In any case, as it stands now, the passage fails to communicate clearly. Can we rectify the situation simply by returning to the singular?

> To any man entered in a National Sailfish Regatta, a woman is a disastrous obstacle. She is forever getting in a man's way.

As usual, correcting the nonsensical error may reveal further possible or even necessary revisions. Here, we could at least use another pronoun if we wanted to:

> To any man entered in a National Sailfish Regatta, a woman is a disastrous obstacle. She is forever getting in his way.

(I also have questions about the precision of "is forever," but that seems somewhat less basic.)

CLEAR REFERENCE

Since pronouns have almost no meaning of their own, every pronoun may attach itself to any number of different nouns, depending upon its context. That means, however, that the writer

must make sure that the pronoun written down actually does refer to the noun or noun phrase he or she is thinking of and not
to some other, similar word or phrase. If the pronoun "agrees"
with *more than one* nearby noun, trouble may result:

> How can a relationship between two people become personal only
> through smiles and other gestures? Without words they cannot fully
> express themselves or learn precisely each other's feelings.

This is a serious pronoun error. After a moment's thought, we
realize that the writer intended for the pronouns *they* and *themselves* to "mean" the *two people* mentioned in the first part of the
first sentence. However, at first reading the pronoun *they* inevitably refers back to *gestures,* which does not turn out to make
sense. (*They* does not refer to *words,* even though it agrees and
is nearby, because of emphasis.)

Something has to be changed here. As usual, the simplest
remedy is to repeat the noun:

> How can a relationship between two people become personal only
> through smiles and other gestures? Without words the two people
> cannot fully express themselves or learn precisely each other's
> feelings.

This will do; the first version will not.

IT, THIS, AND EVERYONE

Several particular pronouns may cause young writers today
special problems.

For one thing, it may sometimes be confusing to the writer
who makes an extra effort to avoid pronoun errors that the word
it, which as we have seen is often a simple pronoun, sometimes
works in a slightly different way, and on these occasions different principles apply. Consider this sentence:

> It is important to avoid pronoun errors.

What does *it* mean? As a pronoun, you would think, this word
should have to be preceded by a singular noun referring to a

thing (not a person) in order to make sense. But this sentence communicates precisely and clearly all by itself; no noun, no anything, precedes the word *it!*

Yes, that is true. When looking over your writing, trying to locate pronouns that might not refer precisely, quickly, and accurately back to preceding words and phrases, do not be confused by this special usage of *it.* Maybe it would be best to think of *it* in such a forward-looking sentence as not a pronoun at all, but more like the word *there* in sentences beginning *"There* is" or *"There* are such and such."

Second, it is also true that the word *this* may sometimes be used to refer to a whole thought (perhaps a sentence or a clause) rather than to a single noun or noun phrase.

<u>This</u> does not happen often, however.

And the word *this,* so used, can often be replaced by a more precise phrase that makes the passage even more communicative. Do not use *this* to refer to a general idea rather than to a single word except in those rare cases where it seems peculiarly appropriate and efficient. Be sure the reference is precise and immediately clear. (You may even want to add a noun after the word *this,* since "this *situation* does not often arise.")

Finally, by far the most common pronoun error appearing in student writing today involves a lack of agreement between *anybody, anyone, everyone,* or *everybody* and subsequent pronouns:

Everyone enjoys themselves.

That sentence, we might as well face it, does communicate efficiently. But it is still not customary to use this phrasing in conventional writing.

Perhaps it simply offends logic too greatly to think that words like "any<u>one</u>" and "every<u>one</u>," which are so obviously singular (how could anything be more singular than *one?*), could agree with an obviously plural pronoun like "<u>them</u>selves." Whatever the reason, it is usual still to consider these words (and the similar word *each*) as singular not only for the verbs they go with but also for all pronouns that later refer back to them.

Everyone enjoys himself

is correct, and only it will get by. If the sex bias in "him<u>self</u>" is wrong in any particular instance, change the whole sentence into the plural—

All people enjoy themselves

—or find some other phrasing altogether.

It is mainly a convention to insist that these words cannot be referred to by a plural pronoun, but doing so can create more serious difficulties on occasion:

> When a society finds someone deviating from the norm, they fear them.

Huh? This sentence is really confusing; not one but two words that seem singular in form but plural in meaning appear in the first clause (from *when* to the comma). Essentially the same pronoun has then been used to refer to two quite different things. The result is not satisfactory.

In this particular case, I believe the difficulty could be resolved simply by considering (as convention would have us do) that "some<u>one</u>" is singular—

> When a society finds someone deviating from the norm, they fear him

—although possibly the relation between *they* and *society* might need tightening up also by saying instead "the *members* of a society *find* . . ."

AVOIDING PRONOUN ERRORS

Some student writers never make pronoun errors. Others are tempted to make them all the time. You have to discover your own tendencies.

If you do sometimes have difficulty with pronouns, your writing is likely to fail its essential task just that often: a pronoun error prevents efficient communication. Fortunately, almost all pronoun errors are easy to avoid, or to eliminate from first drafts.

To be certain you do not leave any pronoun errors on the

pages you have written, read over your next-to-final draft one time looking for nothing but pronouns. You may want to take a blank sheet of paper and hold it under each line, scanning for any and every word that acts as a pronoun—*it, he, she, they, that, this,* and so on. This process will not take more than a minute or so for each page, and it will help you eliminate costly mistakes.

Every time you find one such word, you might ask yourself the following questions:

(1) What is the pronoun's antecedent?

(2) Are both the antecedent and the pronoun singular, or are both plural?

(3) If singular, is the antecedent a "he," a "she," or an "it," and is your pronoun the same?

(4) Does the pronoun refer to the nearest noun it agrees with? If not, are you quite certain its reference is clear? (It may be, depending on the emphasis in your sentences, but you should be skeptical.)

(5) Finally, would each sentence including a pronoun communicate the meaning you have in mind to someone else who does not know you?

You probably do not need to go through this formal list of questions every time. But if you are one of the many writers who have pronoun trouble, you do need to identify every pronoun and its antecedent, and to check whether or not they agree and appear relatively close together. If they do not agree, of course, change one of them so that they do. If they seem too far apart for immediate recognition by the reader, you had probably better repeat the noun or rewrite the whole passage.

Chapter VII

SENTENCES

Language used primarily to communicate information is peculiarly well suited to a distinctly visual medium, the written or printed page. In our time the verbal communication of information is not restricted to the print medium; far from it. We are all accustomed to the communication process that conveys information to us in speech, through radio and the verbal portion of television, as well of course as in that part of our daily lives concerned with the bare exchange of information in conversation with people around us whom we may not know personally.

The errors in student writing today that are most prevalent and yet are elementary enough to threaten the communicative function are all related to the formation on the visual page of that basic unit of meaning, the sentence. In speech (whether purely informative or not) sentences are formed by aural signs, a speaker's pauses and stresses that a listener hears. In writing, as we have seen, these aural signs must be represented visually.

That means that any writer who cares about communicating information must pay attention to *punctuation*.

The Problem

Many students today seem bewildered by punctuation. They have seen all of the basic marks often enough to know what they are: the period, the comma, the dash, even the mystifying semicolon. But in their writing these marks, and the others, sometimes are used arbitrarily, inconsistently. When this problem is pointed out, furthermore, many students seem to feel particularly defensive and uncomfortable. "So what?" their manner seems to say.

I hope you understand by now that there are good, concrete

reasons for a person's being a little out of touch with the basic customs associated with the print medium. It is nothing to feel defensive about. But it does pose a special problem to the young journalist, and—since the ability to communicate effectively in writing is a basic skill useful to anyone, even today—it may well require a special effort to resolve this problem, for all of us.

We must also be sure to distinguish those uses of punctuation that are intimately related to the writer's essential task, to communicate information, from those other uses of punctuation that are primarily matters of convention. Merely conventional uses— as in dates, abbreviations, and footnotes—vary from publisher to publisher, from book to book, from newspaper to newspaper, and so on; sometimes they vary rather noticeably from one to another. Within a single "situation," consistency in even conventional punctuation probably does serve a communicative function. But some uses of punctuation are far more important than these matters of custom. They must concern all writers who wish to communicate effectively.

These uses of the basic marks of punctuation all have to do with the formation of written sentences.

PERIODS

Most sentences are divided from other sentences by a period. Are there other sentence-ending marks? Of course there are! But by far the most common device we have for showing that one meaningful group of words and phrases has been completed and that another is about to begin is the simple period.

This means that it is extremely important *not* to use a period if your sentence is in fact not yet completed.

The "sentence fragment" that would result from apparently ending a sentence "too early" has been called by at least one grammar handbook a sign of outright illiteracy. And indeed it may be, since literacy does have to do with those fundamental devices of verbal communication that are purely *visual*.

Consider how significantly the following "fragment" disturbs the communicative process:

The student council has decided that the annual Halloween dance needs a face-lift. Something challenging yet invigorating, and the winning idea that has been submitted is to have a "Witch and Warlock" Contest.

Try reading that sentence aloud, following the procedures we explored briefly in Chapter III.

The period after *face-lift* makes you think the first sentence has been completed. You pause and perhaps even take a breath. Then you start off on what seems the next sentence and do not realize you have been misled until somewhere around the words *yet invigorating,* where you can see that little comma coming up fast but can find no other words to go along with *Something . . .* that would adequately complete the thought that seemed to have just begun.

Most informational writing, of course, is not actually read aloud. But the eyes of the reader move nevertheless from the first word of an apparent sentence toward what seems its end, grouping words together to form "thoughts." If the eye is misled about where the grouping ends, confusion is bound to result.

The fact of the matter is, in this passage the pause after *invigorating* is even more significant than the one after *face-lift;* yet that second pause is now marked only by a comma, not as "strong" a mark as the period. At least, we must make the following revision:

The student council has decided that the annual Halloween dance needs a face-lift, something challenging yet invigorating, and the winning idea that has been submitted is to have a "Witch and Warlock" Contest.

That will suffice; at least this punctuation now makes it clear, as it was not before, that the thought to be communicated is not completed before it actually is.

"Sentence fragments" are very serious errors. Any writer who has a tendency to use them should learn to eliminate them without delay.

This should be relatively easy to accomplish, since by far most sentence fragments represent, from the writer's perspective, "mere punctuation errors." From the reader's perspective, of course, "mere punctuation" is an extremely significant feature of the communication process, but fortunately, punctuation can be changed easily.

If you discover that you are now and then tempted to place a period in what is in fact the middle of a sentence, take a moment to read over your next-to-last draft looking for nothing else. Cover up all but the words in each sentence, one by one, running from the capital letter to the period. Read each of these apparent sentences aloud to see if it seems complete by itself. That alone should be enough to help you spot any "sentence fragments" you may have written.

If you do locate a "fragment," change the period either before it or at its end to something less conclusive. Try a comma first, and if that does not seem strong enough, try a dash or colon, or even a semicolon. Literally anything would be better than making it seem that a sentence is completed when in fact it is not.

If you still have trouble locating your "sentence fragments," even after reading each apparent sentence aloud, you may want to make use of the old-fashioned definition of what constitutes a sentence: "a group of words, having a subject and a verb (predicate), which expresses a complete thought." Covering up all but the words between your capital letter and your period, locate a noun or noun phrase that is the subject of your sentence and the verb that goes with it that "says" what you are trying to communicate about the subject. That is the easy part.

You will still have to determine if this *clause* (any group of words with a subject and a verb) "expresses a complete thought." To do so, you will have to rely primarily upon your ear and upon what you know you have to communicate.

You may be able to make use of two or three further hints. First, the main way a *clause* is made to express a partial, rather than a complete, thought is easily found at its very beginning. If that thing you are considering a sentence begins with a word such as *when, if, because,* or *although,* or such as *which, who,* or *that,* the chances are good that the thought expressed by that group of words is in fact dependent for its completion on another clause either before or after it. Check and see.

Consider this passage adapted from Chapter I:

Although it is true that the simple conveying of information through the printed word is not as central a part of our culture as it was of our forefathers'. The usefulness of communication skills must still be quite obvious. Most of the ordinary business of our daily, practical lives is conducted by means of the "public language." Whose characteristics we have been exploring.

Let us say that this passage was written by an unfortunate young fellow who had trouble with "sentence fragments." Check this out for him, as I have suggested, covering up all but each section that appears to be a sentence.

The longest "sentence" is that first one, running from *Although* to *forefathers'*. Perhaps it is even long enough to sound complete to your ear; reading it aloud, you would no doubt have to take a breath before going on. But does our definition of the sentence apply?

It is certainly not hard to find a subject and verb here: *it* is the subject, and *is true that* . . . seems to be a long predicate. In fact, all that intervenes between *that* and the period seems to be *"what* is true"; it is all made dependent upon *it is true* by the introductory word *that*.

But just how is this whole clause introduced? Ah yes, *Although* is indeed one of those words that makes the clause that follows incomplete.

Maybe even just reading this passage aloud, you can "hear" that the next section, *the usefulness of communication skills must still be quite obvious,* is necessary to complete the thought begun by *Although.* You may have to take a breath, but if speaking this passage, you would take care to let a listener know with your tone of voice that you had not really reached a true stopping place. In writing, this pause would simply be marked by a comma.

I do not think anyone would be tempted to pause at all, just before the end, between *language* and *whose.* That period is pretty obviously wrong. No punctuation is needed there at all.

The second hint for those few of you who have persistent difficulty with this serious problem of "sentence fragments" is to be especially wary of sentences that seem to end just when another point has been introduced. Here is a classic case, taken from an essay on Albee's *Who's Afraid of Virginia Woolf?:*

The constant arguing throughout the play shows the immaturity of its characters. For example, the argument between George and Martha concerning the moon.

A reader of this passage would expect, naturally enough, that the words *For example* begin a new sentence; the reader would therefore expect a verb to be coming up eventually, after *moon,* to say something about this *argument.* To his or her confusion, the reader discovers too late that what the writer had to say about *the argument* had already been said before the word itself ever appeared.

For the reader, you see, this would be a serious problem. For the writer who discovers the mistake in time, it is an error easily corrected:

> The constant arguing throughout the play shows the immaturity of its characters—for example, the argument between George and Martha concerning the moon.

The pause does seem more significant than the one following the words *for example.* More than a simple comma is necessary, but decidedly not a period, because the sentence is not in fact completed until *moon.*

Another frequent occasion for a "sentence fragment" is the trailing participial phrase:

> I want college to act as an interim between my adolescence and my adulthood. Maturing me educationally as well as broadening and improving my outlook on life.

All writers alerted to the danger of "fragments" would know that the second half of this passage cannot stand alone, wouldn't they? Where is the *subject* of what seems to be the second "sentence"?

COMPOUND SENTENCES

To some students, the phrase "compound sentence" sounds about as frightening as "compound *fracture.*"

In fact, you need not find this kind of sentence painful at all. There is nothing wrong with compound sentences; on the contrary, we all use them all the time. But it is necessary for the writer to identify them as such, so that the reader will not be misled about what to expect in the second half of the sentence, thus threatening the communication process.

A compound sentence is simply two sentences set next to each other, for some reason, in order to make up a single unit between one capital letter and one period. The thoughts expressed by the two sentences would probably be very closely related, but about equally important, to receive this particular kind of stress.

Essentially, we may say, there are two kinds of compound sentence: one in which a little word called a conjunction appears between the two sentences that go together to make up the compound, and another in which the two sentences are merely set next to each other with no particular sort of word in between:

Conjunction: In one kind of compound sentence you will always find a word such as *and* or *but,* but in the other kind you will find no such word.

No Conjunction: There is nothing wrong with compound sentences; on the contrary, we all use them all the time.

Maybe you see already why it is necessary to distinguish a compound sentence from other kinds of sentences, and it should be fairly obvious why it is necessary to distinguish one *kind* of compound from the other. Yes, this too has to do with punctuation.

When the two halves of a compound sentence are joined by a "coordinating conjunction" such as *and, but, yet,* or *for* (and these days, the word *so* seems to me to be used comparably, although this is not a conservative view)—when one of these little words links the two parts of a compound sentence, it is customary to place a comma before the conjunction. We shall see *why* below.

It is important, as we shall also see, when the two halves of a compound sentence are *not* joined by such a conjunction, to place a semicolon after the first "sentence."

Do you see how easy it is to distinguish between the two types of compound sentence? Well, yes, theoretically it is easy. In practice, you may have trouble deciding whether or not the word that comes between the two halves of a compound sentence is a coordinating conjunction or something else. What about words like *however, thus, then, as a result, therefore,* and my own *on the contrary?* Such words and phrases do often appear in the middle of compound sentences. They may be distinguished from conjunctions, however, very easily: unlike true conjunctions, these words *can be moved* without changing the basic meaning of the sentence.

For the student who has difficulty with compound sentences, three questions should be asked about every possible example. First, of course, you must identify the compound sentence: any sentence with more than one group of words having a subject and verb is a possibility. Look at every such sentence and decide if it has two parts each of which could be a complete sentence by itself. (Watch out for "fragments," of course!)

Next, look at all such two-part sentences, and see if you have used a conjunction between the two potentially complete sentences. If you have trouble deciding whether or not a word in between is a conjunction or something else (actually it would be an adverb), then see if you can place that word later in the sentence—before or after the verb, or at the very end. If you can move the word around, it is not a conjunction.

Place a comma before the conjunction when there is one, and a semicolon between the two "sentences" when there is not. We will see why this is absolutely necessary below.

RUN-ON'S

Especially in telling stories, some young writers are tempted to lump so many independent thoughts together in one sentence that a reader has trouble holding them in his mind at the same time without getting confused. A classic example of this is what teachers call "the run-on sentence" (a type of compound):

It was a beautiful night, the moon was full, the air was soft and warm, and everything was quiet and peaceful.

This is just too much "material" to smash all together into one little space between a capital letter and a period. Almost without exception, you should avoid using more than two "possible sentences" simply placed next to each other in a single compound sentence. If you discover such a case in a rough draft, break it up, placing periods where the strongest pauses should be.

It was a beautiful night. The moon was full; the air was soft and warm. Everything was quiet and peaceful.

Despite unfortunately losing the original flavor of the *and,* this does make a considerable improvement on the page. Notice, for example, how the first and last sentences in the revised passage are really different in quality from the two in the middle. The first and last sentences are much more general than the middle two, which may properly remain in one compound sentence.

Sometimes the speaking rhythm—or the writer's thought itself —might quite naturally lead to a run-on:

> The dormitory room had a bare, institutional look, but it was my own and with a little fixing up here and there, I thought it would be fine.

In speech, this might work well. But in writing, without further adjustment of the visual signs indicating "spoken" pauses, the passage does not communicate as effectively as it should. Once again, the problem is that more than two potentially independent sentences have been herded in between a single capital letter and a single period. Try breaking it up some more:

> The dormitory room had a bare, institutional look. But it was my own, and with a little fixing up here and there, I thought it would be fine.

"Merely" adjusting the punctuation in this passage makes it much clearer for the reader.

The Semicolon

A semicolon is never absolutely necessary. A period would always do just as well. A comma, however, would not.

Consider the following compound sentence:

> A horse's temperament depends mostly upon the individual, however the Arab does tend to be more skittish than the Thoroughbred.

This represents a serious error, which would almost certainly threaten the sentence's communicative function.

Notice that we do have a compound sentence. The first section—

A horse's temperament depends mostly upon the individual

—could stand alone as an independent, complete sentence. It has a subject and a verb and has nothing—no word like *if* or *when* or *which* at the beginning, for instance—that would make it depend for its completeness on something else.

The second part of the sentence could also stand alone:

However the Arab does tend to be more skittish than the Thoroughbred—

although when we print it separately that way, it should become obvious that in pronouncing such a sentence, a speaker would pause after *however.* Right? Do you see or "hear" that? It seems a small matter, but it turns out to be very significant.

Maybe the writer of this sentence, a student from Virginia, where horse-training is a favorite sport, identified this as a compound sentence but thought *however* was one of those conjunctions like *and* and *but* that make you put a comma between the two possible sentences in the compound. Can you move *however?*

Give it a try:

The Arab, however, does tend to be more skittish than the Thoroughbred.

The Arab does tend, however, to be more skittish than the Thoroughbred.

The Arab does tend to be more skittish, however, than the Thoroughbred.

The Arab does tend to be more skittish than the Thoroughbred, however.

That represents great mobility indeed. No, *however* is not a conjunction like *and, but, for,* and perhaps *so;* and according to our general principle, more than a comma is necessary here.

But why?

With only a comma before the word *however* in the original compound sentence, the reader's expectation would be profoundly misled. He would naturally expect that the main thought of the sentence's first part was not yet complete and would hurry on to the rest. He would expect, in fact, some phrase like the following:

> A horse's temperament depends mostly upon the individual, <u>however uniform</u> one trainer's experience of a certain species might have been thus far.

Read that aloud next to the first version, now properly punctuated:

> A horse's temperament depends mostly upon the individual; <u>however</u>, the Arab does tend to be more skittish than the Thoroughbred.

See how different the pauses, and thus the sentences' meanings, are?

A very clever person might be thinking that the problem here is really failing to mark the pause after *however,* rather than failing to mark the pause before it strongly enough. But notice that simply putting a comma after *however,* leaving the rest the same, is misleading, too. The reader would expect that *however,* surrounded by commas, was a minor interruption in one continuous sentence:

> A horse's temperament depends mostly upon the individual, <u>however</u>, despite what some writers have said.

Once again, anything less than a semicolon before the second "possible sentence" in this sort of compound will always be seriously misleading.

> There was a long silence, then the priest read the correct answer.

(Some of you may recognize this situation.) The problem is, with only a comma the reader may expect a phrase such as—

> There was a long silence, then a loud noise from outside the room.

If, however, a fully new thought—a possible sentence all by itself—is going to follow the word *silence* here, the reader must be alerted to it. He or she must know to pause more than a mere comma would dictate:

There was a long silence; then the priest read the correct answer.

(Notice again how *then* could appear elsewhere in the second would-be sentence.)

THE COMMA IN COMPOUND SENTENCES

In the other kind of compound sentence, the kind in which a conjunction such as *and, but,* or *yet* joins the two would-be sentences together, it is customary to place a comma at the end of what could be the first sentence and before the conjunction.

Lawrence Riley takes courses at a forestry college, and several national fraternities have invited him to join.

A newspaper must communicate the news clearly and vividly, but not many local papers are written well enough to do this.

These two sentences are now conventionally punctuated. We may wonder how seriously the communication process may have been threatened when the commas were left out of the original papers turned in to me:

Original versions:

Lawrence Riley takes courses at a forestry college and several national fraternities have invited him to join.

A newspaper must communicate the news clearly and vividly but not many local papers are written well enough to do this.

Understanding first clearly what the intended meaning of these compound sentences is and then seeing what was written on the page actually reproduces, of course, the writers' own experience. They knew what they wanted to say; then they looked at what they had actually written down. Should they have been concerned?

Especially in the second sentence, it may seem that these two "original versions" communicate almost as well as the first ones I have printed. And it is certainly true that sometimes leaving out a comma in a compound sentence joined by a conjunction is not really a serious error, but more a matter of custom. However, let us recognize that, here too, the reader may be led by unconventional punctuation to expect a type of sentence that she or he does not actually find. That can always cause confusion.

Without a comma these sentences might lead a reader to expect some phrase like the following:

Lawrence Riley takes courses at a forestry college and several business schools.

A newspaper must communicate the news clearly and vividly but not emotionally.

Just as we noticed in regard to *however* in the example above, the words introducing the second part of these sentences (*and* and *but*) do not by themselves make it clear that a wholly new thought is beginning. A comma preceding the conjunction in such a compound sentence does make that quite clear.

AVOIDING ERRORS IN WRITING SENTENCES

If you do sometimes have difficulty making it clear on the written page where the expression of one thought ends and the expression of another begins, take some time to pay special attention to the way periods normally work in most informational writing.

If you have special *trouble with sentence fragments,* do not fail to make an extra effort to eliminate them right away, since they represent a most serious writing error. Read over your next-to-last draft looking at each group of words you have enclosed between a capital letter and a period. Read each apparent sentence aloud, asking yourself, "Can this stand alone? Does it sound complete?" Be tough on yourself, and when you are doubtful, try a second group of questions on each dubious sentence. "Does this group of words have a subject and a verb?" you should ask, and then, if so, "Is there anything else I have written—an introductory word before the "sentence" such as *because, where, whenever,* or *who,* for instance—that might make this clause depend for its completeness upon another sentence?

Be especially careful of participial phrases, groups of words in which what seems to be the verb is in the *-ing* form; these simply must be "attached" to the sentence either before or after.

Also beware of sentences that end just as something is introduced, which would cause you to write or your reader to expect *for instance* or some other phrase that completes the preparation made by the previous group of words. "And here it is!" That is the kind of phrasing that often tempts young writers to give their readers a false impression of what to expect:

And here it is! A sentence fragment.
And *here* is its counterpart: a complete sentence!

If you have *difficulty with compound sentences,* learn to pick them out when skimming over your next-to-last drafts. Check to see if you have any sentences with more than two clauses that could be sentences by themselves. If so, make some of them into full-fledged sentences.

Check also to see whether your compound sentences are linked together with a conjunction or are simply placed next to each other. Make certain that those not joined by a conjunction are punctuated with a semicolon (or a period). As long as you're at it, you may as well make sure a comma appears before the conjunction in the other kind of compound sentence.

Above all, don't get the impression that punctuation is either insignificant or arbitrary.

Keep clear in your mind which uses of punctuation marks actually affect the communication of information in your writing, by making visual the pauses and stresses you would make in speech. Those little marks are meaningful and systematic devices that the writer must learn to control. Once again, fortunately, the basic principles governing their use are relatively few and relatively simple even in a culture, like ours, that is apparently moving somewhat away from outright domination by the print medium.

Chapter VIII

MODIFIERS

The most embarrassing errors a writer ever makes are modifiers "misplaced" so that they actually change the meaning of some other word than the writer intended. It may be that this problem is sometimes created by inadequate "translation" from speech to writing, since the speaking voice can link together by intonation words that are in fact fairly widely separated. But in writing, without the guidance of a speaker's voice, words group themselves together primarily according to how they appear on the page. Modifiers tend to go with the words nearest to them.

Misplaced Modifiers

It would be bad enough if a phrase that a writer intended to "go with" some other phrase, to make its meaning more precise, were placed so far away that in fact it did not communicate anything. Unfortunately, since in American English word order is extremely significant, modifiers that have been separated from the words a writer intends to associate with them do not simply remain inert. They usually attach themselves to whatever they can find nearby.

Here are three fairly typical examples of misplaced modifiers from essays by my students:

> The poet does not say in so many words that his beloved is beautiful or heavenly, but we can definitely assume that he is very much in love with her throughout the poem, especially in the final couplet.

> The three young soldiers had the grave misfortune of being in the fatal area where two large shells misfired while they were having lunch.

> In the back half of "The Campus Record Shop" is a large, polished tile floor flanked by a row of booths where university dancers can practice a new step or two between classes.

You would think that anyone who had learned to see his writing as it would look to someone else reading it would realize right away that something was wrong with each of these three sentences. In every case, of course, the trouble is that a group of words which the writer evidently intended to associate with one earlier word or phrase becomes associated instead with something else.

In the first sentence, it sounds as though "the poet" is actually loving "his beloved" right there in the poem. The writer probably intended to associate that final section starting *throughout* with the earlier phrase *we may assume.*

> The poet does not say in so many words that his beloved is beautiful or heavenly, but <u>throughout the poem, especially in the final couplet</u>, we may definitely assume that he is very much in love with her.

Now the modifier is properly placed next to the other words whose meaning it should affect.

In the second sentence, of course, the same problem has arisen, perhaps slightly underscored by the unconscious pun *grave,* and certainly complicated by the pronoun *they,* which now refers nonsensically back to *shells.* This is not a question of failing to make sense; it seems to be a matter of making the wrong sense! In this case, the problem may not be solved simply by moving the final clause *while they were having lunch.* Somewhat more revision is necessary.

> The three young soldiers were unfortunately having lunch in the fatal area where two large shells misfired.

Eliminating the unintended pun and converting the verb phrase *had the misfortune* into a mere adverb, *unfortunately,* allows the writer to say what he apparently intended to, but nothing else.

The third sentence could probably be spoken in such a way that it would be clear that "dancers" did not actually "practice a new step or two" in the confined area of a little *booth.* Placement alone now makes the final clause *where university dancers can practice* . . . go with the nearest word, *booths*. It would be possible in speech to separate these two unintended partners with a simple pause. Perhaps in print, a comma would do just as well:

> In the back half of "The Campus Record Shop" is a large, polished tile floor, flanked by a row of booths, where university dancers can practice a new step or two between classes.

By setting off the phrase *flanked by a row of booths* from the rest of the sentence with commas, we might make the *where* clause seem to refer all the way back to *floor,* which the writer must have intended in the first place.

If you think even more is necessary to make this sentence unambiguous, you might notice that the problem arises because we have here two modifiers both of which should go with the same one word, *floor*. Perhaps the writer intended for both modifying phrases, *flanked by* . . . and *where university dancers* . . . , to be of equal significance or emphasis. In that case, we would need a little rewording and somewhat more apparatus for indicating the intended coordination:

> In the back half of "The Campus Record Shop" is a large, polished tile floor, <u>which is flanked</u> by a row of booths and <u>which is used</u> by university dancers to practice a new step or two between classes.

(The first revision with the commas is certainly smoother and does seem to me to be adequately clear.)

BEGINNING MODIFIERS

Writers who have persistent trouble with misplaced modifiers of the sort we find in these three sentences have not adequately learned to imagine someone else, whom they do not know personally, reading what they have written down. They should try reading slowly aloud everything they write for a while, making the effort to imagine this other person. They might even have a friend read their writing aloud to them. In the long run, the best function a teacher or editor often performs is to aid the young writer's imagination in this regard. After seeing the detailed comments a teacher or editor writes upon their own written performances, many students find it very natural and easy to imagine that person (or *some* person) reading every other performance.

A few misplaced modifiers of the embarrassing type will get by every writer during the course of his or her career. But very few of us have persistent difficulty with such grossly misleading "misplacements."

By far the most common misplaced modifiers appear right at the beginning of written sentences. If you remember that modifying words and phrases tend to "go with" those other words and phrases that are closest to them, you can see how the following examples may not say what their writers meant:

If college educated, solely a role as mother and housewife may inhibit the stimulus a woman had received.

As a woman, there is a definite advantage in a college education.

A moment's thought shows us that the writer of the first sentence means to say that "a woman" may be "college educated" and have the experience he describes. But, placed in this order, his words say instead that "a role as mother and housewife" is itself somehow "college educated," which does not exactly make sense, does it?

It is extremely useful, and thus very common, to begin a sentence with a modifying phrase such as *If college educated.* Notice how that phrase allows the writer to communicate a rather elaborate idea with only a few words; spelled out fully, the thought might be phrased, "If a woman has been educated at a college." Yet, properly attached to the following sentence, even the writer's original little phrase, *If college educated,* might communicate just as clearly and efficiently as the more elaborate clause.

But the modifier simply must be placed near the words it is supposed to modify, *a woman.* It would not make sense to move the phrase until later in the sentence; the idea of "being college educated" must be expressed before the words *the stimulus* can mean anything. Since the beginning modifier is so economical, it is best to keep the opening as it is and change all the rest of the sentence so that the words modified immediately follow the opening phrase:

If college educated, a woman may find the stimulus she had received inhibited by a role solely as mother and housewife.

(Notice that the simple modifier *solely* is now also placed precisely next to the words whose meaning it was apparently intended to modify.) It may be that this simple revision, accomplished by merely shifting words about, might reveal to the author of this sentence further revisions he or she might want to make. The whole notion represented by *the stimulus she had received* may now seem unnecessary:

> If college educated, a woman may feel inhibited by a role solely as mother and housewife.

But the most important point to recognize is that, when a sentence begins with a modifier, the word or phrase it modifies must follow immediately. (The phrase modified is almost invariably the subject of the succeeding sentence, by the way.)

My second example quoted above—

> As a woman, there is a definite advantage in a college education

—seems peculiar because no word or phrase appears in the main sentence for the beginning modifier, *as a woman,* to attach itself to. Eliminating the possibly unnecessary words *there is* would merely compound the problem:

> As a woman, a college education is a definite advantage.

But "a college education" is decidedly not "a woman," whatever else it may be. If it seems essential to retain the opening phrase as it is, the rest of the sentence must be completely rethought. Only the writer could do this, of course; but here is the *kind* of sentence we need:

> As a woman, a young person finds a college education a definite advantage.

Now we have what the language requires: a modifying phrase followed immediately by a phrase it may sensibly attach itself to.

As a matter of fact, in this case we might suspect that the writer intended to say something which would dictate a wholly different revision. The modifying phrase itself could be changed into a different sort of phrase altogether, one which does not really attach itself to a single word or phrase at all but which is related instead to the whole of the following sentence. (Some people would say the phrase "goes with" the verb of the sentence, but that would be misleading here, I believe.)

<u>To</u> a woman, there is a definite advantage in a college education.

Notice how, unlike the original beginning modifier, this new phrase can be moved about freely through the sentence (like *however* in the sentences observed in our last chapter) without changing the basic meaning of the sentence.

The beginning modifiers that are likely to create difficulty for the writer are those that cannot be moved this way. When a sentence begins with a modifying phrase of this sort, the word or phrase modified must follow immediately, or the sentence will not communicate effectively.

This kind of beginning modifier may be a simple adjective:

Tall and lanky, President Lincoln physically dominated the visitors. [Decidedly *not:* "Tall and lanky, the visitors were physically dominated by President Lincoln."]

The beginning modifier may be a prepositional phrase used as an adjective (*As a woman* above), or it may be a past participle (*college educated*).

For some reason, however, it seems to be the present participle (*-ing* verb forms) that young writers are most likely to misuse these days:

Besides taking over man's purpose in marriage, most men would feel bad if their wives earned more money than they did.

Getting back to our main subject, women should form a political organization.

Both of these sentences begin with phrases of the sort that modify words or other phrases appearing in the following sentence. It would not make the same sense (if any) to put the beginning phrase at any other position in either sentence. But notice that in both examples, the words which immediately follow the beginning modifiers do not seem to be what the writers intended to associate with them.

In the first example, in fact, we have a very serious error. The sentence on the page actually says something quite different from what the writer apparently meant. How, we might ask, could "most men" take over "man's purpose in marriage"? Once again, we see that, when separated from the words the author intends to associate with them, modifiers have a tendency (at least in writing or print) to associate themselves with those other words nearest to them—even if that does not make sense! It is the writer's job to make sense; the language merely provides a means for doing so. The language must be controlled so that it does communicate the "sense" the writer has in mind.

The first sentence here does not do this, and as a result, it must be changed:

> Besides taking over man's purpose in marriage, many wives would make their husbands feel bad if they earned more money than their husbands did.

In this version, the modified word *wives* does appear, as it must, right after the beginning modifier. This change must be made, unless the beginning of the sentence is itself changed.

The second example is less serious, since in the context of a fairly long essay or editorial, it might serve a useful organizational function. But it does not communicate information efficiently and precisely. The sentence on the page actually says that "women" are "getting back to our main subject." I doubt that "women," as a group, even knew we were talking about them, as this structure seems to imply. Such a phrase will almost always seem awkward in writing. Most basically, it may demonstrate an organizational weakness in the essay as a whole. And second, it also appears to be a misplaced modifier: a beginning participial phrase that is not followed immediately by the noun it modifies.

If such a phrase is absolutely necessary, at the very least the writer should make the sentence itself read meaningfully:

> Getting back to our main subject, let me emphasize again: women should form a political organization.

This revision at least provides a word, *me,* for the beginning modifier to attach itself to, and the whole does make sense.

INCIDENTAL MODIFIERS

Several pages back, we observed a sentence that, even after

the most obvious correction had been made, still might have read as follows:

If college educated, a woman may feel inhibited <u>solely by a role</u> as mother and housewife.

Consider what seems to be the writer's intended meaning in this sentence; and then consider the place of that word *solely*.

In its present position, *solely* naturally "goes with" *by a role,* the phrase coming right after it. Is that, do you think, what the writer means?

In other words, the sentence as it now reads suggests that any number of things might possibly make a woman feel "inhibited" but that "a role as mother and housewife" *is enough by itself* to make her feel that way. In its present order that seems the essential meaning of the second part of this sentence.

But don't you agree that the writer used that word *solely* rather because he or she wanted to stress the limited features of this particular "role"? The intended meaning was not that this role is enough by itself to make a woman feel inhibited, but that a role limited to motherhood and housewifing could be inhibiting. The word *solely* should not really modify *by a role* but rather *as a mother and housewife.* It does not do this in its present position. As we have seen often enough, modifiers attach themselves to the words closest to them if they can. *By a role* is closer to *solely* than *as a mother and housewife,* and in revising this sentence, we should move the modifier:

If college educated, a woman may feel inhibited by a role <u>solely</u> as mother and housewife.

Such a misplaced modifier is not nearly as serious as the grossly misleading sentences we viewed at the beginning of this chapter. It seems even less serious than a beginning modifier that is not immediately followed by the word it modifies in the main sentence. But misplacing even an "incidental modifier" such as *solely* does make our writing less precise than it could be.

It would be hard to call this, for instance, a serious error:

The old man asked me for a dollar, but I only had fifty cents.

But, when you think about it, that word *only* really does not belong with the word *had,* as it seems to. It refers instead to the difference between *a dollar* and *fifty cents.* It is the idea "only fifty cents" that the writer wants to communicate. So why not say that? Or rather, why not *write* it: "I had only fifty cents."

AVOIDING MISPLACED MODIFIERS

Once aware that writers run the risk of misleading their readers by placing modifiers next to words they do not intend for them to modify, most writers are able to avoid misplaced modifiers, even relatively "incidental" ones, fairly easily.

A few young writers today are persistently tempted to begin sentences with modifying phrases which are nevertheless not followed right away by the word or words they are intended to modify. The most common examples of this error begin with phrases structured around a verb in the *-ing* form.

If you are one of those few who do have trouble with misplaced *beginning modifiers,* you should develop the habit of reading over your next-to-last draft one time looking for nothing but sentences that begin, not right away with the subject of the sentence, but with a modifying phrase of one sort or another. Such constructions are not likely to appear with great frequency, perhaps no more than one per page on the average.

Every sentence you discover you have written that does not begin with the subject but with a modifier should be quickly but carefully checked. The modifying phrase beginning the sentence should be followed immediately by the word or phrase you intend for it to "go with." This word or phrase should most often be the subject of the main sentence.

When the beginning modifier is a verb phrase with the verb in the *-ing* form, what you mean to be the "subject" of that *-ing* verb should usually also be the subject of the main verb of the following sentence.

Carefully checking every sentence with a beginning modifier, you will eliminate most of your errors in modifier placement. (Notice how the word *you* in this sentence can be considered the "subject" of both verbs here, both the modifier *checking* and the main verb *will eliminate*).

Chapter IX

CORRECTING YOUR OWN ERRORS

That's about *it*. Seriously!

If your writing "makes sense" in the ways we have studied, if your pronouns work properly and efficiently, if your sentences are adequately marked as such on the visual page, and if your modifiers actually attach themselves to the words you want them to, then you can be pretty sure your writing communicates adequately.

If you discover, either by yourself or by an editor's or a teacher's having told you so, that you tend to have difficulty in a few of these basic areas, then you should now have in mind a fairly simple strategy for avoiding your habitual errors. Read over your next-to-last draft one time, looking for nothing but one type of error common to you as an individual writer. Learn to identify the error, as it has been described somewhere in the preceding four chapters; and try to correct every one you find, using the techniques recommended. Then, if necessary for you personally, read that draft over once more, looking for one other type of error you tend to make, and so on.

ERRORS BUNCHED UP

All of the strategies recommended for avoiding one kind of fundamental error or another are devices for helping you to make sure, more or less at the last minute, that your writing does communicate information adequately. Making yourself especially conscious of your habitual errors at this late stage in the writing process accomplishes two important goals. For one thing, you will feel free *not* to concentrate on "avoiding errors" while you are actually writing, but instead to concentrate on larger matters such as covering all the relevant information, presenting it in a coherent and logical order, and so on. And for another thing, even without explicitly attending to the need to avoid errors as you write first drafts, a little practice in consciously looking for habitual errors in the last-draft stage will tend to shape your *unconscious* writing habits in the first place.

Eventually, you will discover that one or two of your "worst" basic habits will simply disappear.

Unfortunately, one problem that never entirely disappears for any writer is one that probably becomes evident at a middle stage of composition: errors and stylistic weaknesses that appear all run together in the same sentence or two.

In reading over your completed first draft, for the very first time, you will regularly notice that a word here or there needs to be changed; perhaps it needs to be made more precise, more fluent, more accurate or clear. But you will sometimes notice also a whole section, running from a single clause to possibly a whole paragraph, that just does not "sound right." You will learn to check it immediately, of course, for one of your habitual weaknesses; but at least at first, until you have had more practice, you will not notice those truly habitual problems so immediately. You will find them during the final stage of composition (that process of Revision dealt with in Part 4), rather than when you are first reading over the newly completed draft. At this stage you will concentrate primarily on making sure all the necessary information has been covered, in a coherent order, and so on.

Even so, such a passage as I am now thinking of will stand out immediately, even to you (with "all your bad habits"!), as *not quite right*. What do you do then?

Chances are good that such a noticeably rough passage contains several errors and stylistic weaknesses all bunched up. Such a passage is also likely to represent a section of your article that you have not fully thought out yourself. If you yourself do not know precisely what you *want* to say, it is a bit much to expect that your words will say it *for* you. But knowing that, of course, still does not help you revise such a passage, and especially it does not help you revise such a passage quickly and efficiently. Sometimes, in fact often, working on the words will help you work out your thinking.

Faced with a botched-up section like this, you should first make use of the "hierarchy of writing flaws." Instead of simply staring at the offending passage—repeating it over and over silently, aloud, silently again—try running through all the "checks" we have gathered by now; and go through them in the *following order:*

First, check to make sure the passage "makes sense" simply as language: Is there an adjective hiding in the verb phrase? Do all subjects agree with their verbs? (Beware especially of "long subjects" where the true subject of the verb is separated from it by an intervening phrase or where the subject is compound.) Do the verbs' tenses coordinate with each other and accurately reflect the time relation among the events you are referring to? Do you have a word used with another word it normally does not go with, and do your words say, one by one, precisely what you mean?

Second, check to make sure every pronoun (if any) in the passage clearly refers back to a nearby antecedent, with which it agrees in number and gender.

Third, check to make sure your punctuation accurately indicates where the expression of one thought ends and another begins. Is every apparent "sentence" complete? Do you have any compound sentences with more than two clauses that could just as well stand alone? Do you have all compound sentences properly punctuated?

And finally, check to make sure all your modifiers—especially every long phrase that modifies another word or phrase—are placed right next to the word[s] they are supposed to modify. Especially check the relation between any beginning modifier and the word or phrase it should immediately precede.

To run through these four "checks" should take no more than a minute or two for any passage of only one paragraph or less. Some of them will obviously not apply: maybe there are no pronouns to check or no compound sentences. Taking this minute or two to look specifically for these common, basic errors may help you to rewrite the difficult passage without further delay. Perhaps you will spot one or two fundamental problems, resolve them, and that will be that.

But there is a further advantage in having a fixed, orderly procedure ready to apply to any problematic passage in your writing. Taking a minute or two to run through these various checks will allow you to look clearly at what you have written. It will help you to *see* exactly what any reader of that passage would see, nothing more or less. You may well discover in running through the list of checks for basic errors an entirely different sort of problem: an obscure reference that requires clarification, a contradiction, an unwarranted assumption about "what *everyone* knows," or a false assumption that you yourself have been making.

If you discover a botched-up passage in your first draft, if you quickly run through all the checks concentrating on how to revise the passage so that it communicates the necessary information efficiently, and yet you still cannot revise it so that it does "sound right," then scratch out the whole paragraph, reread the article up to that point, glance at what follows if you do not remember it clearly, and start that paragraph all over again using an entirely different beginning.

Never hesitate to rewrite a whole section, from beginning to end, "wiping from your mind" the words you used the first time and concentrating entirely on what information you have to communicate.

Less Serious Common Errors

We have not mentioned every possible error a writer may make. We have not even hinted at every possible error even of that truly fundamental sort that can prevent efficient communication. We *have* touched upon what seem, by far, the most common such errors.

Several other errors are clearly less significant, although they do seriously threaten the communication process, and they appear so often today that they are worth mentioning in closing Part 2.

Possession

If the only factor determining correct usage were what is most commonly done, the little apostrophe (') would clearly be in danger of extinction. But we can be fairly confident that the apostrophe will never disappear, because it does serve a significant communicative function. It serves that function solely, of course, in writing or printing; it is a purely visual communicative device.

Consider the following situation. Suppose a high-school editor has become deeply concerned about the amount of drinking that goes on during official school functions, especially at dances. He feels that some of the resulting behavior is excessive: immature, dangerous, vulgar, and possibly even destructive (the broken bottles and crumpled beer cans littering the parking lot, for instance). Though he feels that the school administrators may be partly to blame for the excessive degree to which standards of prudence and good taste have declined in this regard, the editor believes especially that the students should deal with the degrading situation themselves. As part of his strongly worded editorial, he includes this emphatic sentence:

But let me say this: the problem is the students.

This important sentence would unfortunately fail to communicate the editor's sentiment. In fact, it may well say something he decidedly does not feel. And all this would be true simply because of a missing apostrophe!

The editor "means" that the problem he has been discussing must be dealt with by the students themselves; the problem is *theirs*. But he has said, in fact, that the students *are* the problem. This would be a much more serious charge.

But let me say this: the problem is the students'.

That is what he intends to say. In this case, and potentially in every case, the difference between a simple plural and a possessive may be crucial to the communicative process. It is the apostrophe that distinguishes between the plural -*s* and the possessive -*'s* or -*s'*.

Of course, there is one exception to this general principle; and its exceptional quality causes another of the most common, only sometimes serious, errors found in student writing today: the confusion of *its* and *it's*.

The apostrophe is most often the sign of the possessive, rather than the plural; as a result, when many students need to use the possessive of that little pronoun *it,* they quite naturally use the apostrophe: *it's.* Unfortunately, that means something different. The apostrophe is used to denote the possessive only with nouns. Unlike nouns, pronouns have plural forms which are not made by adding *-s.* The plural of *it* is *they,* for example. The possessive forms of pronouns, which are made by adding *-s,* therefore, do not need to be distinguished from anything else. The possessive form of *it* is simply *its,* just like *his.* [*It's* means "it is," a so-called contraction that many style manuals say is not appropriate to formal writing anyway.]

COMMAS: PAIRS, WITH MODIFIERS, WHEN NEEDED

Besides the general principle we have already observed about the comma in compound sentences, most students get along quite well with merely the general principle in mind that a comma represents a slight pause. But on three or four occasions, an additional comment or two might be helpful.

For one thing, many students recognize that it is customary to pause briefly before any of the many kinds of interpolated phrases we use all the time, such as: *for example, of course, in fact, on the contrary, I think, by the way, according to . . . , as a result,* and so on. Our language includes thousands of such phrases that we use to link our sentences together and to make our writing read more smoothly. In addition, we have many precisely comparable single words, such as: *however, therefore, then, incidentally, besides,* and so on. Yes, we do usually pause before such incidental words and phrases, since they do not often contribute directly to the flow of the sentence's own movement.

The point to remember is that we usually pause *after* each of these expressions also.

Sometimes, furthermore, we set a word or phrase apart from the sentence's ordinary flow in order to emphasize it, especially, more than the other words. The point to remember there too is that we usually pause both before *and* after such an emphatic expression. Many a comma that is used to indicate a brief pause is, in fact, one of a pair of commas *both* of which you should take care to put down on the page. I doubt that it could be considered a serious error if you left out the second of such a pair of commas, but if it is significant to mark the first one, it should be equally significant to mark the second.

Long modifying phrases are often set off from the main part of a sentence by a comma, or by a pair of commas if the phrase does not appear at one end of the sentence or the other. All of the examples of "beginning modifiers" we looked at in the last chapter seemed to require a pause before the subject of the sentence itself. This comma usage hardly ever causes difficulty for anyone.

Long modifying phrases that appear at the end of sentences (or clauses) may also need to be set apart by a comma, and one type of "trailing modifier" does sometimes require a comment. The pronouns *this* and *which* are slightly freer than most pronouns. Their reference, sometimes (and only when you are careful), may be a bit looser and more general than the reference of the other pronouns. In an earlier chapter, for example, I quoted this sentence (now properly punctuated):

My father hit me, which is hard to take.

The original version of this sentence had a period after *me.* The writer clearly recognized that a strong pause was necessary there; indeed it is. With no pause, or rather with no mark of punctuation, it would almost seem that the word *which* was supposed to refer back to *me,* this being hard to understand.

A period here would create a sentence fragment. A comma is sufficient. Situations like this rather often arise, the comma helping to free a pronoun such as *this* or *which* from referring to the noun or pronoun nearest to it.

For the record, perhaps we should also state here again that some pauses do not require a comma, nor do they require anything else. It is normal to pause slightly between the main elements of every sentence: between subject and verb and between verb and complement. The pause between subject and verb is sometimes quite considerable, especially if the subject is fairly long in itself and especially if the verb one "finally" gets to is just *is.* Such a pause is so standard that a reader does not need to have it marked specially for him; it might even be confusing. (But when you know a pause would be necessary in speaking your sentences intelligibly, do not neglect to use a punctuation mark unless you are quite sure it is *not* needed.)

Also, some writers want to emphasize their moving from one

thought to a contrary one by saying *But* quite emphatically at the beginning of a sentence. As a result, they write: *But,* . . . . This comma, too, is unnecessary and possibly confusing; the reader would expect one of those interpolated phrases such as *But, on the other hand,* . . . If emphasis is the only reason for such a pause after *yet* or *but* at the beginning of a sentence, change that word to the more emphatic *however,* which usually is surrounded by pauses.

Today's Most Common Misspelling

Most teachers may not have had the same experience as I have had, but I am myself constantly surprised at how often students these days write *then* when they mean *than.*

Perhaps young people today pronounce these two different words the same?

In any event, even a mere misspelling can seriously threaten communication. (It once took me several days, for example, to understand what a simple description of a "saw-tring iron" was about. You know: *"soldering* iron.") And the use of *then* after *more* or *-er* instead of *than* is more serious than mere misspelling since *then* is a word in its own right, with a set of meanings quite different from *than.*

In such a minor matter, as in all the other more significant matters we have surveyed in this Part 2 on Correctness, only a conventional or "correct" usage *can* communicate information efficiently.

It remains to be seen how a writer may make sure his "correct" usages are also "effective" ones.

PART 3

Effectiveness

Chapter X

THE FIVE ESSENTIAL FEATURES
OF EFFECTIVE WRITING STYLE

Writing designed primarily to communicate information efficiently must have certain features in order to accomplish its purpose. Any departure from these necessary conventional patterns of word order, usage, and even punctuation may be considered an "error" preventing communication. But conventional patterns are not enough alone to insure that writing communicates information effectively. The patterns a writer uses must do more than "sound good" or "look nice" on the printed page. They must also be *meaningful*.

In other words, you must take care that your sentences conform normally to habitual language patterns, but also that they *say* precisely what you *mean*.

Departures from meaningfulness of this sort could not exactly be called errors, partly because only you could know precisely how the sentences you have written correspond to the meaning you intend. But it is possible to describe stylistic "weaknesses" that are likely to diminish the capacity of a writer's sentences to communicate information effectively.

REVISION

As we have seen, a writer must always feel free to revise what she or he first writes in order to make sure it communicates effectively. Sometimes the revision process will reveal areas in which the writer has not yet figured out precisely what he wants to say and so will provide a genuinely basic improvement to the written work. Sometimes revision will be necessary simply to eliminate an unconventional sentence pattern or punctuation usage that might confuse the communication process between writer and reader.

But even more often, a writer looking over an early draft will change a word here, a phrase there, perhaps one or two whole sentences, in order to improve the "effectiveness" of the writing *style*. The original phrase may not correspond precisely enough to the information the writer needs to communicate. It may seem inefficient, taking many words to "say" what could be communicated in only a few. Or it may seem merely awkward.

You should be alert to passages in your writing that, although correct by conventional standards, do not seem to you to communicate meaningfully, rapidly, and clearly. As always, you must feel free to scratch out an offending word, phrase, or sentence, and start it all over again. If it seems only a single word at first that is uncommunicative, try to change it. If a moment's thought is not enough for you to substitute a more meaningful term, try changing the phrase or the whole sentence in which it appears. Try several different versions you might think are attempts to "say" the same thing. Pronounce them aloud if that helps. Do anything that aids you in making that phrase or sentence communicate effectively. But do not leave it alone, if you can help it. As always, you should concentrate in the revision process, as in the original composition, upon the information you want to communicate.

FIVE ESSENTIAL FEATURES

In American English, the most efficient written communication is active, decisive, concrete, objective, and specific.

An *active* sentence carries much of its meaning in its verbs, including all verb forms such as participles, infinitives, gerunds, and so on. In effective writing, verbs are *active* instead of passive: "someone *does* something" instead of "something *is done.*" *Active* sentences do not usually include *being* verbs: "someone *does* something" instead of "something *is* such and such." As we shall see in the next chapter, sentences with a predominance of nouns ending in "-tion" or "-ment" should especially be revised, with the long nouns converted into *active* verbs.

Inactive: Written communication is essential to society.
Active: A society needs to communicate in writing.

A *decisive* sentence does not "beat about the bush." It says what it has to say boldly, clearly, and unhesitatingly. *Decisive* writing does not rely on simple modifiers; it remains unqualified. An odd fact about American English is that often what seems to be intensifying words such as "very," "quite," "particularly," and so on, turn out to weaken a phrase in the long run, rather than making it more emphatic.

Indecisive: One might say that there are certain possible differences, which are very important, between spoken and written language.
Decisive: Writing differs significantly from speech.

Concrete language is the opposite of "abstraction." Writing that is *concrete* includes many examples from actual experience; it is practical, down-to-earth. In effective writing of this sort, the reader can often see, hear, or feel in imagination the experience being described. The information being communicated is "brought home" or "made real."

Abstract: Reading aloud is often helpful in the revision process.
Concrete: In revising, a writer might try reading his or her first draft aloud.

Objective writing concentrates on "what" is being communicated rather than on "who" is writing or reading the communicative language. We often think of *objective* statements as the opposite of "subjective" ones, but this may be misleading. For one thing, it is often impossible (and undesirable) to separate "objective" from "subjective" thoughts. Perhaps it is more useful to contrast *objective* writing, which concentrates on what is communicated, with "emotive" writing, which either expressly appeals to an audience or expresses the personality of the writer.

Emotive: A person who cannot properly control his writing, his language, has no functional control over his very thinking, over his undisciplined mind itself.
Objective: Language is intimately related to thought.

Sentences that are *specific* communicate more effectively than "generalizations." To make a point effectively, the writer often cites a *specific* example illustrating or supporting his general idea. Writing that deals exclusively in generalities is dull, vague, hard to imagine. Writing that is *specific,* on the other hand, is often vivid, well defined, even sometimes exceptionally effective.

> *General:* Many students finishing high school today have considerable difficulty writing correctly.
>
> *Specific:* "Roland," a typical student, wrote a descriptive essay that included many common errors in syntax, pronoun reference, and punctuation.

Many of these desirable stylistic traits naturally go together. Writing that includes many *specific* examples, for instance, is almost automatically *concrete. Objective* writing, which also tends toward the *concrete,* may tend to be *decisive* too. It may even seem natural for many writers to deal with *concrete, specific,* and *objective* matters in sentences that are *active* and *decisive.*

The first step toward effective writing is to learn to recognize clearly these five essential features.

The second step, which we shall discuss at length in the next chapter, is to know *how to revise* the "inactive," "indecisive," "abstract," "emotive," and "general" writing that you may find here and there in your own stories and articles.

"Concise" and "Precise"

Somewhat more generally, effective communication in writing might also be described as both "concise" and "precise."

Redundancy, or simple repetition, and "wordiness" often are actually confusing in informational writing. The writer should strive to say what he or she has to communicate, one time, as clearly and straightforwardly as possible. If the communication seems imprecise, vague, or unclear, then those sentences should be scratched out and rewritten more effectively.

In speech, of course, we do not "scratch out" anything. If we say something that seems vague or unclear, we add another sentence or two, trying to communicate the same thought but more *precisely.* In informational writing, however, the reader expects the expression of one thought to be followed by the expression of another, different one. Any variation of this expected pattern, unless it is explicitly "signaled" (by a phrase such as *that is* or *in other words*), will almost certainly confuse the communication process.

The writer looking over a first draft, incidentally, should be suspicious of even properly "signaled" repetitions; they may indicate that the writing of that whole section is not as economical as it should be. Instead of saying *that is* or *to reiterate,* maybe the writer should look again at the first attempt to communicate this thought to see whether or not the original statement could be made more *precise* and the second statement could be eliminated altogether, which would make the whole section more *concise.*

COMMUNICATION IS MOST IMPORTANT

Let's face it: it is easy for me to say that your writing should be concise and precise, and that your style should be active, objective, and so on. It may even be relatively easy for you to distinguish generalities from specifics, concrete statements from abstractions, and so on. But even so, it is not always easy to make your own writing actually have these most desirable qualities.

The communicative writer sometimes feels he is confronting two, unfortunately opposed facts about his or her profession. It is a fact that in American English, the most effective written communication is usually active, decisive, concrete, objective, and specific.

But it is also a fact, a quite obvious one to any practicing writer, that all "meanings"—all information, all ideas or thoughts—do not have all these qualities, or perhaps even any of them!

The best we can do is to make sure our writing has as many of these qualities as possible *without sacrificing accuracy.* Above all, your writing should communicate the information you have to convey as accurately, as precisely, as clearly as possible.

When it is necessary, unfortunately, to choose between "stylistic excellence" and accurate communication, the informational writer of course must choose accuracy. A sentence that is awkward but clear will do; a sentence that is fluent but meaningless will not.

Chapter XI

COMMON WEAKNESSES IN WRITING STYLE

A word or two about ego might be in order here. It is hard not to feel personally involved with those little marks you as a writer put down on the printed page. For some people, in fact, the most difficult obstacle to overcome in learning to look at their writing as it would appear to someone else is created by their own pride. They feel proud of the words they have thought of or the way the words look on the page. The writing seems to express the writer himself or herself perfectly, or to be sure to impress every reader.

The informational writer, of course, cannot afford this particular kind of vanity. Rather, you as a journalist should take pride in how well you are able to *revise* your writing, improving the degree to which it communicates information effectively. Not only must you be "thick-skinned" about comments from your editor or writing teacher, but you must also be able to scrutinize your own writing coolly and critically.

Keep in mind at all times the dictum that informational writing does not EX-press, nor does it IM-press; it simply communicates.

ACTIVE AND INACTIVE WORDS

One of the most common, and debilitating, temptations we seem to face these days, especially when we are dealing with complex or abstruse material, is the seductiveness of big, impressive nouns and weak *being*-verbs. Not only young writers confront this temptation; all writers may be so tempted from time to time.

Consider the following passage:

A proper appreciation of the significance that one can have in protecting his immediate ecosystem is necessary for each and

120

every person, so that he may consciously determine the destiny of his environment.

This is not a simpleminded nor an insignificant statement. It presents no problem of correctness, since all the normal patterns we expect of our language are properly reflected. Unhappily, we may even be familiar with this general manner of speaking or writing.

The style is just not very efficient or communicative. Look especially at the combinations of subject and verb:

one can have significance in protecting . . .
appreciation is necessary for . . . every person
every person . . . may determine the destiny of . . .

The final clause, *so that he may consciously determine the destiny of his environment,* is indeed general and possibly even abstract. But it is not excessively emotive, and it is decisive and active. It seems concise and precise.

But it is also quite different from almost all the rest of the sentence! The impersonal *one* is vague and abstract, whenever it is used; to *have significance* is at least an awkward, unclear expression; and *appreciation is necessary* is extremely vague. The problem with this sort of writing might be described as an unsatisfactory coordination between word and "idea." What we might normally consider a *"verb* idea"—a thought involving an "action" rather than a "thing"—seems often expressed here with a *noun.* This is a common weakness in writing that appears designed more to impress an audience than to communicate information. (Politicians and other salesmen often talk this way.)

Notice that *appreciation* is really a kind of action, and that even the expression *is necessary* might be thought to say something about the "act" of *needing.* Also, the word *significance* expresses a thought more often expressed by a modifier, *significant* or *significantly.*

The most basic construction here is this: *A proper appreciation . . . is necessary for each and every person.* To begin properly sorting out what we might think of as "verb ideas" and "noun ideas," we had better start with this most basic unit. Our goal is to make more apparent the active "idea" somewhat hidden in the word *appreciation.* Hopefully, we can find some form of the verb "to appreciate" that will communicate the meaning intended. The related notions expressed originally by *proper* and by *is neces-sary* must surely be taken into account; and of course, the whole notion about "significance" has to be communicated also. The stress upon *each and every person* seems basic to the writer's intention too.

To make such an ineffective passage active, precise, and clear, we should look for a subject-verb combination that communicates the intended meaning but in an active or dynamic manner. It seems clear in this case that *each and every person* should be the subject, and that some form of *appreciate* should be the verb. To communicate the part about "being necessary" we might say "needs to appreciate." To retain the idea expressed by *proper,* however, we could say *"should* appreciate," which might include and surpass the idea of *need,* making it superfluous.

> Each and every person should appreciate the significance he can have in protecting his immediate ecosystem, so that he may consciously determine the destiny of his environment.

Already that seems a considerable improvement. The sentence as a whole is more active, concise, and decisive. The awkward *one* construction has been eliminated.

But the vague business about "having significance" still remains. According to the general principles of effective writing style, we should try to throw more emphasis on the active part of this component in the sentence, the verb form *protecting.* The word *significance* might better be transformed into a modifier, if we can do that while still expressing the basic intended meaning.

Notice that the writer apparently wants to stress how much every individual can contribute to environmental protection. Perhaps we might convert the rather lame, inactive phrase *"in* protecting" into a full, active clause: "how significantly he can protect . . ." That is perhaps stronger than the intended meaning; slightly softened, our final revision might read as follows:

> Each and <u>every person should appreciate</u> how significantly he can help to protect his immediate ecosystem, so that he may consciously determine the destiny of his environment.

Simply by converting "overactive" nouns into active verbs with simple subjects, this revision makes the original passage considerably clearer and more effective. (Notice also that the revised, active passage is six words shorter than the ineffective, inactive original.)

Converting Nouns into Verbs

Stylistic weaknesses that "sound impressive"—such as using long nouns with inactive verbs—are surely the most difficult weaknesses for a writer to revise in his own writing. Similar problems in coordinating word and "idea" occur all the time in anyone's writing, but most of them will immediately seem wrong unless they have this oratorical ring flattering to the writer's ego.

If your writing tends to be heavy and rhetorical, rather than active and informational, then you had better learn to spot passages in your first or second draft that look like this:

> In Malraux's novel *Man's Fate,* there is a continuous reenforcement of the notion of isolation.

Like all constructions using *one,* many uses of *there is* or *there are* are likely to be ineffective. The phrase in itself is both inactive and vague.

But an even more revealing sign of stylistic weakness in this sentence is its use of a noun as a basic sentence element that seems to express a "verb idea." Nouns ending in *-ment, -tion,* or *-sion* may usually be suspected of "hiding a verb idea." Notice how vague the word *reenforcement* is: who or what "reenforces" the sense of *isolation* the novel is said to convey, the author? the novel itself? Eliminating the relatively empty *there is* reveals this imprecision quite clearly:

> In Malraux's novel *Man's Fate,* the notion of isolation is continuously reenforced.

The passive *is . . . reenforced* is less wordy than the *there is* form, and in this case it seems about equally emphatic. But the sense of who or what is doing the "reenforcing" as well as whose "notion" is "reenforced" is still left vague. Could we just eliminate the indirect connection at the beginning?

> Malraux's novel *Man's Fate* continuously reenforces the notion of isolation.

This does not seem ideal; saying "to reenforce a notion" does not seem to fit normal usage exactly. But at least we have improved the degree to which this sentence communicates actively and decisively. The author of this sentence, who alone knows what she originally meant, could now perhaps revise the wording further.

This kind of stylistic weakness, substituting inactive forms and long nouns for active verbs, is so common and so ineffective that one more example may be called for:

> The enlightening incident, although it was perhaps meaningless to anyone other than myself, gave me some assurance that my conclusion about dishonesty never being a good idea was valid.

A phrase like *other than myself* is by itself a sign that the writer of this sentence was concerned about using language "impressively" or maybe "politely" rather than simply and efficiently. Why not just say "anyone but me"?

Such a revision is not in itself terribly significant, but a phrase like that may call your attention to a whole passage in your writing that could be improved, as this sentence certainly should be.

First things first: the clause, *my conclusion about dishonesty never being a good idea was valid,* includes a fairly elementary error. Notice that the *conclusion* is not "about" just *dishonesty;* rather, the *conclusion* is "about" a more complex concept than a single word can represent. The original phrasing is wrong; it must be changed to this:

> my conclusion about <u>dishonesty's never being</u> a good idea was valid.

Adding *'s* to *dishonesty* is a necessary means of linking together that whole phrase saying what the conclusion is "about."

But the style of this passage is still awkward and ineffective. Once again, the problem lies in the inactive form of the sentence. Notice how many words in the sentence express what might be considered "verb ideas": *enlightening, assurance, conclusion, was . . . meaningless, being a good idea, was.* But notice how all the *active* "verb ideas" are expressed by forms other than verbs, the verbs themselves being used to express various kinds of "being." The writer of this sentence should have tried to make some form of *to assure* and *to conclude* the basis of the last section of his sentence.

> The enlightening incident, although it may have had meaning for no one but me, <u>assured me</u> that <u>I had been right to conclude</u> that dishonesty is never a good idea.

RELATED SIGNS OF INACTIVE WRITING

We have seen that the impersonal *one,* sentences depending on *there is* or *there are,* and long nouns (often ending in *-ment* or *-ion*) hiding "verb ideas" may all be signs of inactive, unclear, generally ineffective writing style. Several other constructions often function the same way; when you find any of them in your first or second draft, you should be alerted to the possibility of stylistic weakness. Try to identify a genuine "verb idea" in the meaning you intend to communicate, as well as a specific someone or something that may be correctly made into the subject of the "verb idea" properly expressed as some form of an active verb.

There is or *there are,* sometimes effective ways to control emphasis in speech, may often be eliminated from written passages with very slight revision. *One* should be changed for a precise, specific subject whenever possible; if this is impossible in a particular instance, try using a term equally general but a little less vague such as *a person* or *an individual* (*a writer, a student, a gambler,* or some such phrase would be even better). It may be possible to convert the whole sentence into the plural. Even a passive may read better than the stilted *one* construction, though a passive is inactive by definition and also a bit vague. Nouns that seem to express "verb ideas," as we have seen, should be changed if at all possible into genuine verbs.

Two other phrases sometimes appear in passages of inactive, rhetorical, but incommunicative writing: *in that* and *due to the fact that.* If you should find these awkward phrases in your writing, you might inspect the passage in which they appear for inadequately precise, decisive, specific, and active wording. These linking words do not in fact indicate precise connections among thoughts. Their use may suggest that you have not thought out exactly what you want to say.

For a good many years the phrase *due to* was not accepted at all in standard American English either as a conjunction meaning *because* or as a preposition meaning *because of* or *by*. Teachers used to say that *due* is an adjective:

The delay in the baseball game was <u>due</u> to rain.

Teachers would have approved that sentence, but not this one:

The baseball game was delayed <u>due to</u> rain.

This, the rule went, is an "improper" way of saying *because of* or *by*.

By now the language has clearly changed enough so that the use of *due to* as a conjunction or preposition is acceptable. But you might bear in mind that *because* or *because of* is certain to communicate efficiently and clearly, even when *due to* may not be.

And, speaking of certainties, you can be absolutely sure that every use of *due to the fact that* takes five relatively meaningless words to communicate what *because* says in only one:

> *Original:* In college, <u>there</u> is a tendency for <u>one</u> to behave with fellow students' actions in mind as a model, <u>due to the fact that</u> many live in close proximity to each other in dormitories.
>
> *Revised:* A college student tends to model his or her actions after the behavior of fellows students, because many live close together in dormitories.

(Notice that leaving *actions* and *behavior* as nouns here is not ideal, since they may be thought to express "verb ideas." At least the worst signs of awkwardness, inactiveness, and imprecision have been eliminated.)

The phrase *in that* is worse. Posing as a device to link two thoughts together with the second logically dependent upon the first, the phrase in fact usually "says" nothing at all. Either it hides a more precise relationship, often clearly expressed again by *because;* or it pretends to make an explicit logical connection where only an implicit one exists in fact.

Hidden Cause: The Board's proposal is inadequate, according to

> the SC President, <u>in that</u> it does not take the students' wishes into account.

It would be more precise and decisive to say <u>because</u> here, claiming in effect that the inadequacy of the proposal "is <u>caused</u> by" its failure to respond to students' wishes.

> *Fake Relation:* The Board's proposal is inadequate, according to the SC President, <u>in that</u> the students will not accept it.

This may or may not be a causal relation. Placing a semicolon after *President* and deleting *in that* would place these two statements side by side, leaving their relation implicit, as it should be, without wasting empty words.

Probably every writing teacher could add to this list of phrases and constructions that are ineffective almost every time they appear.

To avoid all of them, try to keep all your writing active, precise, and economical; and keep clearly in mind that your goal is just to communicate information as plainly, simply, and clearly as possible—not to impress anybody with your own personal attributes.

AWKWARDNESS

Just conceivably, writing may be active, decisive, concrete, objective, and specific, and still fail to communicate as effectively as possible. Such a passage would be "all right" but not "great."

Consider this sentence:

> An hour before the party, the students rearranged the furniture in the rec room and put some folding chairs around so that people would have where to sit and enough room to walk around without having to climb over furniture or people.

Perhaps the general idea is communicated fairly well here, but the sentence grows more and more awkward as it proceeds. The final clause, starting *so that . . . ,* seems especially ungainly. "People *would have where . . .*" may not be exactly an error, but it seems close to it. Trying to make *where to sit* and *enough room to walk around* equal or parallel also seems inelegant and rough. (We shall see more on "parallel structures" in a later section of this chapter.)

When you find an awkward passage such as this in your first or second draft—and you will: everyone does now and then!—check it first for an elementary error; then, if you find none, it might be best to rewrite the sentence as a whole. In this case, the only relatively minor revisions I could suggest would produce the following sentence:

> An hour before the party, the students rearranged the furniture in the rec room and put some folding chairs around so that guests would have <u>something to sit on</u> and <u>enough room to walk around in</u> without having to climb over furniture or other guests.

At least the rhythm of this version is somewhat improved.

The most common kind of awkwardness appearing in student essays these days may be an injudicious use of clauses beginning with *where, when, who,* and the like.

> The puppy had tape on his ears <u>from when</u> he was clipped.

> The priest's most enjoyable trip <u>was where</u> he met an Irish rabbi.

Such sentences are used fairly often in conversation, perhaps to place emphasis properly; but they seem awkward in writing.

This kind of phrase may mask a more precise connection between thoughts:

> The puppy had tape on his ears <u>because</u> he had been clipped recently.

Or it may indicate, once again, an inadequately active sentence:

> On the priest's most enjoyable trip he met an Irish rabbi.

If you ever discover a clause like this, beginning with an interrogative word like *how, when,* or *where,* following a *being*-verb or a preposition, rewrite the sentence. It may communicate adequately, which is what counts most, but it is almost certain to seem awkward, which is not ideal.

VAGUENESS

Avoiding too many abstractions and keeping your sentences active should eliminate from your writing the most damaging kind of vagueness. Consider this passage:

> Humanity is estranged from its authentic possibilities. The basic vision prevents us from any unequivocal view of the sanity of common sense, or the madness of so-called mad men. Perhaps we may see the conformists as the insane ones and society as the institution.

You might think the context surrounding this apparently strongly felt assertion would make its meaning clear. Unfortunately, that is not true: one whole page of this student's essay reads just like this passage. What does it all mean? *The basic vision? Perhaps we may see . . . society as the institution?* Perhaps?

Such an extreme failure to communicate is not likely to appear in your writing if you strive at all times to write as much as possible in active, decisive, concrete, objective, and specific language. But once in a while, you may discover a less serious example of vagueness. In the sentence quoted above about the student party in the rec room, the writer originally referred to *people* who would be coming to the party. That word is much less precise than we might hope for in effective writing. At least we might say *guests* or *party-goers*. In all such cases the writer may know, from the story as a whole, some bit of information that would allow an even more precise expression.

In this instance, students were throwing a party for honored members of the faculty. Instead of saying *guests* and certainly instead of using the extremely vague *people*, the writer could have said *faculty invitees* or something else equally definite. Whenever you see an extremely general or vague term in your writing such as *people, things*, or any form of *some* ("*some*thing," "*some*where," "*some*one"), see if you can find a more precise term instead.

WORDINESS

Wordiness is inefficient, by definition. Using more words than necessary to make an idea clear may show off a person's extensive vocabulary, but it does not communicate information effectively. Compared to an elementary error or to one of the most basic stylistic weaknesses we have discussed such as inactive or abstract phrasing, wordiness is not a serious defect unless, like an extreme case of vagueness or awkwardness, it leads to lack of clarity. But wordiness is easily remedied, and eliminating it always makes your writing more effective.

In extreme cases, wordiness may prevent communication altogether:

The most essential component of a door, that by which a structure comes to be classified as a door, is the mass or frame of the device itself. The structure can be of almost any kind of rather unyielding, durable material. A door can be of any size or shape, though it is usually rectangular. Doors are almost always quite small in breadth, relative to their length or width.

The young man who wrote this passage some years ago, and left it unrevised, is now an older man embarrassed by it (me!). This paragraph is part of the "meaningless verbiage" I referred to in Chapter II. It takes so many words to say so little that it is actually unclear.

For one thing, just look at all the modifiers: *most essential, almost any, almost always; rather, usually, quite.* "*Most* essential" is repetitive in itself, and then still another statement of "what is essential to door-ness" follows in the awkward *that by which* clause. If the second one is necessary, then the first one surely is not. And so the paragraph continues.

If you should ever discover such a wordy passage in your writing, scratch it out entirely. Reconsider the purpose of the paragraph in relation to the essay or story as a whole, and rewrite the paragraph as plainly and succinctly as possible. Don't look at what you have scratched out.

It is much more likely, however, that you will occasionally find passages in your writing like the following sentence:

The Hooper Report shows clearly the definite need for mental institution reform.

Clearly and *definite* are not both necessary for communicating information. The writer probably used both words because he wanted to be especially emphatic. In itself, such a desire to appeal to the reader's emotions is suspicious in informational writing.

Besides, the writer might discover that converting the nouns in this sentence that seem to express "verb ideas" into genuine verbs would communicate more emphatically than his repetition of two similar terms:

The Hooper Report shows clearly that mental institutions need to be reformed.

PARALLEL PHRASES

One noticeably awkward but still common stylistic weakness arises from inadequately balancing what could be parallel phrases (or "parallel structures," as they are often called). Here are several examples of inadequately balanced phrases:

Whether or not a man is deaf, dumb, or he just does not know a language, he is not disqualified from being able to express what he feels.

The language of advertisers is hard-hitting, concise, and stated in such a way as to make them sound truthful.

An ad must not only be eye-catching by its color, position, and design, but also by the words in it.

Not only has the American woman changed in her role as wife and mother but also politically.

In the first two cases, we have phrases in a series not all of which have the same form. This results in awkwardness. The general idea is communicated fairly clearly in each instance, but the sentence does not read smoothly.

In any series, or in any pair of parallel phrases, whether they are linked by *and* or by *or,* the phrases should be parallel in form if at all possible. Usually, a fairly minor revision can turn the trick:

Whether or not a man is deaf, dumb, or just ignorant of a particular language, he can still express what he feels.

The language of advertisers is hard-hitting, concise, and apparently truthful.

The third and fourth examples make use of the effective balancing device, *not only/but also*. . . . But in each instance, these incidental modifiers are misplaced so as to be imprecise, and the form of what follows is not parallel.

In the third example, *not only* does not really "go with" the words that follow, *be eye-catching*, but with the long *by* phrase further along. In the fourth example, similarly, *not only* does not "go with" *has . . . changed*, as it seems to, but with *in her role*. . . . Once again, we must be sure to make the phrasing parallel in both instances:

An ad must catch the eye <u>not only oy its</u> color, position, and design, <u>but also by its</u> words.

The American woman has changed <u>not only in</u> her role as wife and mother <u>but also in</u> her political role.

The writer who has learned to place his incidental modifiers precisely next to the words whose meaning they are intended to affect should have no trouble placing *not only* and *but also* correctly. The next step is to make sure the phrases these paired modifiers qualify have the same general form.

(Incidentally, when *not only* correctly begins a sentence, it may be considered to modify the main verb. Often the next sentence, or the second half of a compound sentence, will not include the usual *but,* even at the beginning, and the usual *also* will appear later, along with the verb:

<u>Not only</u> is it necessary to place these modifiers meaningfully; it is <u>also</u> effective to make the phrases that follow them parallel in form.)

WRONG WORDS

A student in Creative Writing once wrote the following speech for a central character, as his one-act drama reached a moment of high emotion:

"Ralph, please! *Please* don't take me for granite!"

This is probably an extreme instance of the wrong word being used instead of what was actually meant (*granted,* you know).

But the same kind of thing can happen in less extreme degrees to any writer, especially if he or she does not take care to say exactly what is meant as plainly and directly as possible and to match as precisely as possible the words on the page with the information to be communicated.

Here are several examples of wrong words:

Jean-Paul Marat insisted that only by revolution could the people destruct the hierarchy of power in the monarchic system. [The word intended is *destroy;* "destruct" exists as a verb only as part of the combination "to self-*destruct.*"]

The young man was afflicted with a skin disease which he contracted while habitating in the cellars of the city. [The writer means simply *living;* even "inhabiting the cellars . . ." would seem stilted.]

A dictator continually poses his ideas on the people. [The word is *imposes.*]

Dr. Meyer believes that GNP, the total value of goods and services produced in a country, gives a good inclination of where the economy is going. [*Indication* is the word the writer is thinking of.]

Most of the patients emitted into the hospital are there on a voluntary basis. [The word intended in this inactive, wordy sentence is *admitted.*]

According to their teachers, after a few weeks of intensive reading, students usually become more curious of the world around them than they were before. [An error in "normal usage" that, strictly speaking, does not make sense, although the general meaning intended seems clear: "curious *about*" is the usual combination.]

Sometimes, it is true that a person's own individual language does not precisely correspond to what we have been calling "the public language," and some "wrong words" inevitably result from this discrepancy.

But it seems clear to me that some of the examples here—at least that peculiar formulation, *habitating*—result from the writer's desire to use an "impressive vocabulary" rather than simply to communicate information efficiently.

No doubt others—perhaps including the obvious mistake, saying *inclination* instead of *indication*—result from the writer's not paying enough attention to the visual aspect of his writing, failing to see the written words as they will look to an unknown reader. A few "wrong words"—perhaps *emitted* instead of *admitted*— seem unavoidable, but they will tend to disappear with increased experience in both reading and writing.

If you discover that you do have a tendency to use words mistakenly, try strengthening your ability to *see* your writing in the ways discussed in Part 1 of this book. Keep in mind at all times that your job as an informational writer is not to impress someone with your extensive vocabulary but merely to convey information as efficiently as possible. And when you are reading other people's writing, be alert to words and phrases you are not altogether familiar with; keep a good dictionary handy at all times, and look up all of the unfamiliar words you find.

One final suggestion: *burn your thesaurus*, if you have one. (Or rather, sell it to a used-book store!) A book of synonyms, so long as it is arranged by semantic categories and not merely by the alphabet, can be useful on very rare and highly specialized occasions. But for most young writers, a thesaurus is almost certain to do more harm than good. Never use any term with which you are not thoroughly familiar. To do so would invite you to use words mistakenly, and no one will ever be "impressed" for long by a "wrong word"!

Writing merely in order to communicate information may seem a rather humble task. Perhaps it is. But a writer who can do so *well*, who can communicate even complex information *effectively*, may take justifiable pride in his or her ability to perform successfully a role that is essential to our society.

Chapter XII

IMPROVING YOUR OWN STYLE

A journalist always writes under time pressure. In fact, no writer is ever entirely free of all need to finish his or her job quickly.

On the other hand, no writer can ever be certain that the marks she or he has put down on the visual page will adequately communicate to someone else, until he or she has looked at them carefully, taking the time necessary to make them more "correct" (if necessary) and more "effective" (if possible).

Obviously, these two facts about the writer's task jar against each other. Writers often feel they never have enough time to make their writing as effective as they could, given sufficient time.

THE IMPORTANCE OF REVISION

It is particularly essential for the student writer to make the time necessary to revise his or her first draft carefully and patiently. After very little experience, you should be able to determine how your own writing tends here and there to be "incorrect" and learn to spot your "errors" and correct them efficiently. In a similar manner, though perhaps a bit less simply, you can determine how your writing style tends to be "ineffective" and, hopefully, can learn to locate weak spots quickly and revise them without too much difficulty.

Making this effort now, and making it again whenever you can throughout your writing career, will pay enormous dividends later. When writing your first draft, you must feel free to concentrate on "covering" all the information, putting your story or essay into a coherent, logical form, performing successfully the job you have been assigned. But then, after you have done that satisfactorily, you need to make sure all your sentences communicate as you intended them to, both correctly and effectively.

Of course, you must eliminate any departures from the basic language habits of your readers. And, of course, the more you can make your language effective, rather than just adequate, the better—for you, for your editor or teacher, for your readers.

Making such an effort, consciously and conscientiously, now and whenever possible, will help to shape your unconscious habits later *as you write your first draft.* The frequent "errors" will eventually disappear as your own habits become more attuned to conventional ones; the incommunicative stylistic weaknesses will also tend to appear less often and less disastrously. But, whenever you can, and especially now at the beginning of your writing career, you have to take the time and make the effort to revise both for correctness and for effective writing style.

REVISING FOR STYLE

Style is such a complex coordination of meaning, phrase, specific assignment, experience, and even personality that we cannot devise a perfectly simple system for revising first or second drafts in order to improve their style. Some young writers discover that they have an easily identifiable stylistic habit, such as a tendency toward long nouns and weak verbs, which they can look out for in revising all their articles and stories. But even such basic stylistic habits are likely to vary according to the particular subject matter the writer is dealing with on a particular occasion.

The best procedure for looking over the style of your early draft is just to keep generally in mind the most basic principles for effective writing in American English. Usually, the most communicative writing in our language is—

ACTIVE, focusing on vivid, dynamic verbs;
DECISIVE, avoiding too many (weak) modifiers;
CONCRETE, never abstract except when absolutely necessary;
OBJECTIVE, not appealing to an audience's emotions or directly expressing a writer's own; and
SPECIFIC, illustrating all generalizations with concrete and particular examples.

You should try to spot departures from this type of style in your own writing, as well as in that by others.

In Part 4, we shall explore the revision process I would recommend for one particular rough draft, applying the strategies for insuring "correctness" introduced in Part 2 as well as these basic principles for effective style that we have been studying in Part 3.

In the remainder of this chapter, it may be useful for you to consider several more paragraphs from student essays, selected more or less at random, comparing the originals with the revisions I propose. These passages do not include many outright errors, but all of them need considerable rewriting to make them communicate effectively, perhaps even more revision than I suggest here.

A STYLISTIC SAMPLE CASE

Original:

The day finally came when I received a letter of acceptance from one of the colleges of my choice. My family was happy for me, and joined me in the excitement of my new experience. Then was the time for more serious thought and planning. I looked to my parents for financial aid. After my family and I had computed our budget we were faced with the hard, cold fact that there would not be adequate funds for me to continue my education at that time. However, I was determined not to be beaten. I knew what it was that I wanted to do. Ideas about putting myself through school entered my mind. . . .

Suggested revision:

One day I finally received a letter of acceptance from one of the colleges I had chosen. My whole family was happy and excited for me. But a little later, we had to think and plan more seriously. I looked to my parents for financial aid, but after we had computed our budget we were faced with the hard fact that we would not have enough money for me to continue my education at that time. Still, I was determined not to give up. I knew what I wanted to do. I thought about putting myself through school. . . .

Original:

The essential parts of a belt are a piece of leather and a buckle. This particular belt is a size 38; it is 41¾ inches long, not including the length of the buckle, and ¾ of an inch wide. There are two ends to a belt. This belt was shaped to form a point at one end. Approximately 2 inches from the point there are five holes, each ¼-inch long and ¹⁄₁₆-inch wide. They lie an inch apart from each other. The leather at the opposite end is folded over the center bar of the buckle serving the purpose of keeping the buckle in place. The leather is being held down by a double-headed nail. The buckle . . .

Suggested revision:

A belt has two essential parts: a long, thin, flat piece of leather and a buckle. This particular belt is a Size 38; not including the buckle, it is 41¾ inches long, ¾ of an inch wide, and [?] of an inch thick. Approximately 2 inches from one end, which is pointed, are five vertical slashes, each ¼-inch high and ¹⁄₁₆-inch wide, set an inch apart from each other. At the opposite end, the leather of the belt is folded over the center bar of the buckle and held down by a double-headed nail, to keep the buckle in place. The buckle . . .

Original:

The most memorable part of my trip to Israel is when I first set my eyes on the *Kotel* (the Western Wall). . . . Being in Israel that summer and visiting the Wall was not only a learning experience, but a maturing experience. I learned that religion can keep a person going on without materialistic things in Israel (probably other places if one tried) and to have faith in something—to believe in life itself.

Suggested revision:

(NOTE: In the context of the original essay as a whole, this passage does not seem as vague and sentimental as it may appear to when printed by itself.)

What I remember most vividly from my trip to Israel is the first time I saw the *Kotel* (the Western Wall). . . . From traveling in Israel that summer and from visiting the Wall, I not only learned; I also matured. I now know that religion can keep a person going on even if he or she lacks material [comforts?]. I have learned to have faith, to believe in life itself.

Original:

To advertise usually means promoting something in order to sell it.

Suggested revision:
To advertise means to promote a product in order to sell it.

Original:
During the Civil War, the North had a direct plan of attack. The plan included a naval blockade, a division of the Confederacy in half by the Mississippi River, and a second wedge through the heart of the South. Southern strategy, however, was not coordinated. The South had no basic plan of attacking the North from the beginning until the end of the war.

Suggested revision:
During the Civil War, the North had a well-defined plan of attack, which included three major objectives: using the Navy to block [Southern seaports?], using the Mississippi River to divide the Confederacy in half, and using [Sherman's troops?] to drive a second wedge through the heart of the Old South. Southern strategy, on the other hand, was not coordinated. Throughout the war, the South had no overall plan of attack.

Original:
(NOTE: This sentence appears in an essay about several male characters in a war novel.)
If a man's personal destiny is an integral part of his entire being, wouldn't it stand to reason that his actions, also an integral part of the entirety, dictate quite a bit of importance, even in the shadow of mortality?

Suggested revision:
If a man's destiny as an individual helps to define his very identity, then doesn't it stand to reason that the actions he takes [during his lifetime], which also help to define his identity, retain great significance even when he is about to die?

Original:
On Sunday almost all people are active in sports, social events, or work on their lawn and house.

Suggested revision:
On Sunday almost all [adults in the town?] actively participate in sports or social events, or in work on their lawn or house.

Original:

As an audience, one begins to almost pity Estragon and Vladimir [in Beckett's play *Waiting for Godot*]. This might be due to the fact that they need and depend on each other so very much. It is very frustrating not to have anything to do with one's life and therefore have to invent words which have no special meaning but just to pass the time.

Suggested revision (including correction of two *elementary errors*):

Estragon and Vladimir depend on each other so much that the audience may begin to pity them. They have nothing to do with their lives, which must be frustrating, and therefore have to invent words which have no special meaning but which merely pass the time.

A CONCLUDING NOTE

In the long run, only you can revise your own writing. Others, like me, can only make suggestions, since you alone know what you want to "say."

Perhaps the best we "others" can do is to show you what active, decisive, concrete, objective, and specific writing looks like.

The rest is up to you.

Chapter XIII

THE ROUGH DRAFT

After interviewing a local biology teacher about her recent trip to Europe, a student journalist returned to her school newspaper's office and worked up the following draft of a feature story.

One Word Says Much

"Most Americans take freedom for granted," according to Ms. Elizabeth L. Pool, Senior High biology teacher who has just returned from a trip to Czechoslovakia, "until they see what it's like to live without it."

Ms. Pool and her husband, a tax consultant, traveled to Europe for about six weeks. Some of the countries they visited were England, France, Austria, Germany, and Czechoslovakia. This trip was not only a new and exciting one for the Pools, but it was also very educational. "We saw so many things I never dreamt we would, and I learned so many things it was as if a dream had come true," Ms. Pool said recently.

Czechoslovakia was one country Ms. Pool found particularly striking. It brought to her attention some things she never thought about or merely took for granted.

The first city which was visited by Mr. and Ms. Pool was Prague, or, as some people call it, "The City of the Thousand Towers". Prague, according to Ms. Pool, is a city of diversity and beauty. Most of the castles, cathedrals and churches have stood through eleven centuries, witnessing the many changes it underwent. Today, Ms. Pool notes that these majestic structures hover over the modern houses, offices, apartment buildings, parks and subway.

In appearance, the whole country is beautiful but, the Pools discovered, this beauty is superficial. Upon seeing the country's inhabitants, one can see that something is missing; one immediately notices that a very essential factor is lacking, Ms. Pool said. Every since 1945, Czechoslovakia has been an Iron Curtain country, thus, people have been deprived of the greatest gift a nation can own - freedom; the people literally have no rights. For example, they do not have the right to own a house, choose a career, or permission to go traveling in any country outside the Communist domain. Most important, however, they do not have the freedom of speech, religion, or press:

The people, according to Ms. Pool, can not express their thoughts publicly. It is unheard of to criticize the government. While, in a free nation, one can speak what is on one's mind and either praise, or disapprove of the country's governing body.

The people, Ms. Pool learned, may practice the religion of their choice, however, in doing so, they become ostricized by the government. While again, in a free nation, one can be a Catholic, Protestant, Jew, Buddhist, Lutheran, or whatever one pleases without fear of any intervention from the government.

Finally, in Czechoslovakia, all means of communication (radio, television, newspapers, magazines) are controlled by the government, and therefore, a very limited amount of and only government-selected material can be broadcasted or printed. Any foreign news which the government feels does not agree with their principles or way of thinking, will not be published. This is not ture in other, free nations; different means of communication are owned and controlled by different companies or individuals.

These are just a few examples of some rights we take for granted, without realizing that there are many nations around the world who do not know what these rights mean. In speaking with some of the people in Czechoslovakia, adds Ms. Pool, it is obvious that before the Communist take-over, Czechoslovakia was a peace-loving country with a very stable and satisfying government. The people were very content and worked very hard to better themselves and their country. After the Communists took over Czechoslovakia, the people have no desire to improve themselves or the country because they know that they would not benefit from the improvement at all, rather, it would only be the government which would gain more recognition and strength.

One doesn't appreciate the value of freedom and the ownership of certain rights until he/she sees or feels the lack of it elsewhere, Ms. Pool's experience would indicate. It is unfortunate indeed that human nature works this way but she thinks that if one is not fortunate enough to visit countries such as Czechoslovakia, one can still learn to appreciate what he/she has by just stopping a moment and thinking about what freedom really means and how different our way of living would be if we were deprived of it . . . if we would just put a little more thought into that one word that says so much: *Freedom*.

Let us say that the young woman who wrote this story has spent most of her time and effort so far organizing the wealth of material she had gathered in her hour-long interview with Ms. Pool into a coherent and interesting essay. This process might take several drafts by itself, of course.

She now has just enough time left before her deadline to revise the article carefully and, if necessary, to retype all or parts of it. She must make certain, of course, that her story communicates accurately, but also correctly and effectively.

Chapter XIV

REWRITING IN THREE STAGES

If the writer of "One Word Says Much" had had very little experience, she might feel trapped by what she had already written. She might know that her main objectives had been accomplished and that she had not written any sentence without concentrating on saying what she meant clearly and meaningfully. Looking over the rough draft, she might only be able to recognize the results of all her earlier decisions about organization and even about word choice.

The more experienced writer, however, will have learned to look at what he or she has written as it will look to someone else. This gives the writer a slightly changed perspective, revealing features of the rough draft that might not have been obvious otherwise. The experienced writer will be able to proceed at this stage in an orderly and efficient manner.

THREE READINGS

First, of course, the writer of "One Word Says Much" should make sure the article "makes sense" in a general way, checking for coherence, logical development, and so on. When dealing with a complex subject, a writer may have to rewrite a whole essay at this stage.

After that process has been completed, if necessary, we may say we are looking at the "next-to-last" draft. At this stage, the writer of "One Word Says Much" would look for those errors she is prone to, those language habits she has developed that depart from the customs of a wider, more "general" public. In this case, the writer knows that she has a tendency to mark her sentences

144

and independent clauses incorrectly, using commas, semicolons, and periods idiosyncratically and thus confusingly. She has also had some trouble now and then with pronouns.

Finally, in revising the rough draft, the writer should make sure the style is clear, meaningful, precise, and concise. Wherever possible, the sentences should be active, decisive, concrete, objective, and specific. This particular writer has a tendency to discuss feature material, such as what we find in this essay, in a style that is sometimes awkward and wordy, perhaps in a desire now and then to "sound impressive" rather than simply to communicate effectively.

[After whatever retyping is necessary, of course, the writer must look carefully at the new copy to eliminate any typing errors.]

GENERAL REVISION

I hope my own readers will agree with me that, in general, "One Word Says Much" is interesting, coherent, and effective. Concluding the article by returning to the idea expressed in the direct quotation right at the start seems especially clever, tying the whole neatly and meaningfully together.

This much the writer would note and approve as she first looked over her rough draft. Two somewhat less basic features should also be noted, however, which disturb the general coherence.

At the end of the fifth paragraph, the student has written that the Czechoslovakian people "do not have the freedom of speech, religion, or press." Yet elsewhere she speaks of the city's churches and later even says, "the people . . . may *practice the religion* of their choice." Such a contradiction does not make sense; it should be noticed early in the revision process and either eliminated or resolved.

In this instance it seems clear that the contradiction is caused by imprecise phrasing rather than fuzzy thinking. After saying in the later paragraph that the people may indeed practice religion, the student notes immediately that they are penalized for doing so. The fact seems to be that Czechoslovakians do have a certain degree of religious freedom, but not a truly meaningful one. Rather than eliminating the phrase saying that they do not have any religious freedom, we might try for a more precise expression.

Maybe the sentence should read that the people "do not have freedom of speech, freedom of the press, or *a truly substantial freedom of religion."*

(Once when I suggested a similar revision to make another student's sentence more precise, he commented that now the modified sentence was *wordy.* He was mistaken, as I tried to demonstrate. The informational writer simply must use as many words as are necessary to communicate accurately; doing so could never be called *being wordy.* The writer whose goal is to communicate information efficiently simply cannot afford a type of verbal economy which is achieved at the sacrifice of accuracy. I suspect that in fact my student liked the way his original sentence "sounded." It had a pleasing rhythm to his ear, and of course, revision broke up the rhythm. But the informational writer cannot afford to write primarily for "sound effects"!)

The second general problem in "our" first draft may be harder to resolve. It appears in these two sections:

Every since 1945, Czechoslovakia has been an Iron Curtain country, thus . . . the people literally have no rights.

. . . Before the Communist take-over, Czechoslovakia was a peace-loving country with a very stable and satisfying government. . . .

Before writing this story, perhaps before interviewing Ms. Pool, the reporter should have familiarized herself with recent Czechoslovakian history. That is merely sound journalistic practice. Such a general knowledge would make a reader wonder if Ms. Pool was thinking here, as the wording implies, of "the Communist take-over" in 1948 before which Czechoslovakia in fact had had a "stable government" for less than three years; or if, on the other hand, she was thinking of the much more recent Russian invasion, which has reversed the previous trend in Czechoslovakia toward greater democracy and civil freedoms. This fairly recent conflict did not set Communists against non-Communists, however.

Perhaps Ms. Pool must be consulted again. In any case, this apparent inaccuracy must be eliminated.

HABITUAL ERRORS

After these general adjustments have been made, the slightly revised draft of "One Word Says Much" should be read for those elementary errors that the writer has learned she rather often makes if she is not careful. First, she knows that she has a tendency to punctuate her sentences improperly; so she must read the draft one time, looking at every group of words beginning with a capital letter and ending with a period, to make sure it is a complete sentence. At the same time, she needs to identify every compound sentence and check its punctuation.

SENTENCES

This reading should reveal altogether at least seven basic errors. The second quotation from Ms. Pool looks suspicious, for instance:

"We saw so many things I never dreamt we would, and I learned so many things it was as if a dream had come true," Ms. Pool said recently.

Ms. Pool herself was speaking, of course, rather than writing; the punctuation here is the writer's attempt to translate Ms. Pool's oral stresses and pauses into visual signs.

Punctuated as it is now, the quoted passage looks like an ordinary compound sentence: two independent clauses joined by *and* with a comma at the end of the first clause. But look again. Could we indeed place a period where the first comma now appears?

We saw so many things I never dreamt we would . . .

No, because of that little modifier *so,* this thought is not completed until the very last part of the quoted passage, *it was as if a dream had come true.* The writer is certain, however, that a pause is necessary after *would.*

Notice that not one but two clauses here depend for their completeness on that last section. As a result, whether we have a comma after *would* or not, we must have one after *things:*

. . . I learned so many things, it was as if . . .

The last section must be separated from the clause just before it so that the reader will know it has an equal relation to both of the preceding dependent clauses:

"We saw so many things I never dreamt we would, and I learned so many things, it was as if a dream had come true," Ms. Pool said recently.

Several paragraphs further on, the following sentence also needs to be scrutinized carefully:

Every since 1945, Czechoslovakia has been an Iron Curtain country, thus, people have been deprived of the greatest gift a nation
can own - freedom; the people literally have no rights.

As we have seen, this sentence may need revision for its historical content, but its form also needs review. The student who knew she needed to watch out for improperly punctuated compound sentences would certainly pick this one out for revision. She would note immediately that not one and not two independent clauses are grouped together between this one capital letter and the one period; *three* clauses are jammed together.

The passage needs to be broken up further, into at least two separate sentences. That means that either the comma after *country* or the semicolon after *freedom* must be changed to a period. Let us say that the writer prefers to change the semicolon. Now we need to look again at the compound sentence that would still remain:

Every since 1945, Czechoslovakia has been an Iron Curtain country, thus, people have been deprived of the greatest gift a nation
can own - freedom.

Incidentally, looking at this sentence for its basic punctuation, the writer might notice the typing error, *Every* instead of *Ever;* and she might change her peculiar form of dash to the more conventional form, *can own—freedom.*

More significantly, of course, she would need to decide which kind of compound sentence she has. Is it the kind in which the two independent clauses are joined by *and, but,* or another of those immobile conjunctions? *Thus* appears to be the linking word, but notice that it can be moved:

· · · people have <u>thus</u> been deprived . . .
· · · people have been deprived <u>thus</u> . . .

No, more than a comma is necessary to separate the independent clauses in this compound sentence:

> Ever since 1945, Czechoslovakia has been an Iron Curtain country; thus people have been deprived of the greatest gift a nation can own—freedom. The people literally have no rights.

Looking over the major punctuation of every sentence in her rough draft, the student would also notice the following passage:

> It is unheard of to criticize the government. While, in a free nation, one can speak what is on his mind and either praise, or disapprove of the country's governing body.

The first part of this looks fine; the section between the capital letter in *It* and the period after *government* seems complete all by itself.

But what about that section appearing to make a second separate sentence?

> While, in a free nation, one can speak what is on his mind and either praise, or disapprove of the country's governing body.

This, despite the punctuation, is not a complete sentence. *While* is one of those conjunctions that make the clause that follows dependent for its completeness upon some other independent clause (in this case on the sentence before). The original version of this section, in other words, included a sentence fragment; it must be revised this way:

> It is unheard of to criticize the government, while, in a free nation, one can speak what is on his mind and either praise or disapprove of the country's governing body.

(If the writer is disturbed by the three commas that appear quite close together here, the one following *government* could be made into a semicolon. But it cannot be a period!)

Similar revision of sentence punctuation is required throughout the essay. From this point to the end, three other compound sentences are now improperly punctuated, and two other passages are now sentence fragments.

PRONOUNS

In the past, pronouns have also given this particular student some trouble. She needs to scan the rough draft once again, this time looking only at pronouns.

The first passage to catch her eye may be another quotation from Ms. Pool. The last line of the lead paragraph now reads as follows:

". . . until _they_ see what _it's_ like to live without _it_."

Three pronouns appear in this line, all of which should be checked for clarity and precision of reference.

They refers back to the first words of the story, *Most Americans*. Although that phrase is not really close to the pronoun itself, no other noun intervenes to which the pronoun could refer either grammatically or meaningfully.

But the student would probably notice that the two *it*'s appearing so close together do not refer to the same thing. The first one is not really the usual sort of pronoun requiring an antecedent; the second refers back to *freedom* in the first line. The student might be wary of such a long interruption between antecedent and pronoun, especially since the problem is complicated by that repetition of *it*. A simple solution might be to put Ms. Pool's statement back together:

"Most Americans take freedom for granted until they see what it's like to live without it," according to Ms. Elizabeth L. Pool. . . .

The two *it*'s remain unchanged in this revision, but the reference of the second one is now so unambiguous that the whole passage reads clearly and effectively.

Quickly locating and checking pronouns, the writer would proceed through several more sentences, approving four or five pronoun uses. Then, she would notice this sentence.

Most of the castles, cathedrals and churches have stood through eleven centuries, witnessing the many changes _it_ underwent.

The entire paragraph in which this sentence appears talks about Prague, and the writer ceertainly knows that the *it* here should refer back to *Prague* in the preceding sentence. But the separation between pronoun and antecedent is fairly great; maybe the noun should be repeated.

At least two other pronoun errors also need to be corrected later in the draft. The student may note as she ends up her pronoun review that several pronouns may not function properly in the last paragraph. But that important passage clearly needs some stylistic improvement also, after which it may be checked again for "correctness."

THE THIRD, DETAILED READING

Now that the student has quickly read over her article, verifying its general sense and coherence and eliminating her customary errors, she may feel reasonably confident that her essay communicates *adequately*. But she cannot yet feel certain that no incidental errors appear here and there, marring the clarity of one or two passages; nor can she feel sure that every sentence communicates as *effectively* as possible. She needs to read it one more time, but this time looking at every detail: reading each sentence patiently, trying to *see* it as it would look to someone else, and attending to just how well it communicates her precise meaning.

In this reading, since she has already eliminated what are most likely to be her own most common errors, she may feel free to change anything, major or minor, that does not seem exactly "right."

For example, the following sentence certainly communicates clearly, but it may seem a little strange:

Ms. Pool and her husband, a tax consultant, traveled to Europe for about six weeks.

Do you see what the somewhat awkward expression is? We do not usually say "to travel *to*" someplace "for" a certain amount of time. Logically, that would imply that the voyage itself took that long without saying anything about how long the travelers stayed. "To" should be changed to *in*.

Next, we might notice this sentence:

This trip was <u>not only</u> a new and exciting one for the Pools, <u>but</u> it was <u>also</u> very educational.

This compound sentence has already been checked for its punctuation and for its pronouns. Perhaps in looking at those possible trouble spots, the writer may already have noticed the slight imprecision of the *not only/but also* phrasing. The writer knows that usually the phrases following these terms should be in a parallel form. But *a new and exciting one* is a different sort of phrase from *also very educational.*

A moment's thought might reveal that the original sentence is actually wordy. (What does *one* add to the meaning of the first clause?) Eliminating the wordiness balances the phrasing:

> This trip was not only new and exciting for the Pools, but it was also educational.

That seems both more economical and more emphatic. (If she wanted to, the writer could also make this passage more *active:* "The Pools found this trip not only new and exciting, but also educational.")

The next sentence to catch the writer's eye certainly should be this one:

> Czechoslovakia . . . brought to her attention some things she never thought about or merely took for granted.

Bear in mind that the student is now scrutinizing each of her sentences, making sure that every one successfully communicates her meaning precisely and effectively. Taking this hard-nosed approach, she should be able to spot here the imprecision in her verbs' tenses. *When* did the "thinking" and "taking for granted" occur compared to *when* the "bringing to her attention" took place?

> It brought to her attention some things she <u>had</u> never <u>thought about</u> or <u>had</u> merely <u>taken for granted</u>.

The same problem recurs several sentences further along:

> Most of the castles, cathedrals and churches have stood through eleven centuries, witnessing the many changes Prague <u>underwent</u>.

Obviously, Prague "was undergoing" these *changes* at the very same time the buildings "were standing" there. The second verb *underwent* should be changed to the same tense as *have stood.* (Also, on this reading the writer may wonder what the difference is between *cathedrals* and *churches.*)

> Most of the castles and cathedrals have stood through eleven centuries, witnessing the many changes Prague <u>has undergone.</u>

As a matter of fact, wordiness seems a consistent danger throughout the essay. The following passage is typical:

> In appearance, the whole country is beautiful, but the Pools discovered that this beauty is superficial. Upon seeing the country's inhabitants, one can see that something is missing; one immediately notices that a very essential factor is lacking, Ms. Pool said.

The second sentence here surely needs some cutting:

> On seeing the country's inhabitants, the visitor immediately notices that an essential factor is lacking, Ms. Pool said.

As in this passage, all other instances in the text of wordiness involving *very, one,* and simple repetition should be rewritten more economically. The writer should pay attention to the style of her concluding paragraph in particular. (In this case once again, the writer may also decide to make her sentence more *active:* "the visitor immediately notices that their lives lack an essential factor, Ms. Pool said.")

As she works through her draft this final time, the writer would no doubt make several other changes, which might include the following:

> . . . there are many nations around the world who do not know what these rights mean.

Is "knowing a meaning" really the issue here? The writer seems to want to stress that the citizens of "many nations" do not have comparable basic rights, but her phrasing may wander from this original intention. Perhaps the following version is more precise:

> . . . Many nations around the world have nothing comparable to these rights.

Another passage which certainly should be rewritten is this one:

> For example, they do not have the right to own a house, choose a career, or permission to go traveling in any country outside the Communist domain.

This sentence should seem awkward to anyone. After a moment's thought, perhaps the source of the awkwardness may be identified as, once again, a problem with parallel phrasing.

Own a house and *choose a career* both have a similar form and rhythm; but *permission to go traveling* . . . is quite different, even though these seem to be three phrases in a simple series. An easy revision is possible:

> . . . the right to own a house, to choose a career, or to travel to any country outside the Communist domain.

Just as certainly, the following passage also requires revision:

> In speaking with some of the people in Czechoslovakia, Ms. Pool adds, it is obvious that before the Communist take-over, Czecho-slovakia. . . .

The problem here may have disappeared in the general rewriting we discussed several pages back. But if the sentence still has this form, some change is needed.

Notice that *In speaking* . . . is a beginning *-ing* modifier; we know that the "subject" of the *-ing* verb should also be the subject of the main verb. *Ms. Pool adds* is merely an interrupting phrase unrelated to the main sentence (as you can tell from the fact that it can be placed almost anywhere without changing the basic meaning of the sentence). No, this is the main sentence: *it is obvious that.* . . . Either the beginning modifier or this main sentence must be changed in order to eliminate the simple error:

> In <u>speaking</u> with some of the people in Czechoslovakia, Ms. Pool adds, a <u>visitor</u> learns that. . . .

Finally, the last paragraph surely deserves some attention:

> One doesn't appreciate the value of freedom and the ownership of certain rights until he/she sees or feels the lack of it elsewhere,

Ms. Pool's experience would indicate. It is unfortunate indeed that human nature works this way but she thinks that if one is not fortunate enough to visit countries such as Czechoslovakia, one can still learn to appreciate what he/she has by just stopping a moment and thinking about what freedom really means and how different our way of living would be if we were deprived of it . . . if we would just put a little more thought into that one word that says so much: *Freedom*.

This significant paragraph is consistently awkward and wordy. The last sentence in particular seems quite an empty appeal to the reader's emotions.

The paragraph deserves careful study, sentence by sentence:

One doesn't appreciate the value of freedom and the ownership of certain rights until he/she sees or feels the lack of it elsewhere, Ms. Pool's experience would indicate.

The basic device using *one* and "he/she" is so inelegant that it is positively distracting. Also, does a person "own civil rights?" That seems like a "wrong word."

I have suggested in Part 3 that whenever you encounter a wordy, awkward *one* phrase in your rough draft, you should try to find a more precise expression. Do you think Ms. Pool is thinking here of "Americans" in particular, or of "citizens of all free nations"? If so, instead of *one* we could say, *"An American* does not appreciate . . ."* or *"A citizen of a free nation* does not appreciate . . ."* At the very least, we could say *a person* or *an individual*.

Notice also that *it* here may seem to refer to two nouns, *freedom* and *ownership,* which would mean that a plural pronoun is required:

The citizen of a free nation does not appreciate the value of freedom and of civil rights until he or she sees the lack of them elsewhere, Ms. Pool's experience would indicate.

That seems much improved. Instead of a rather ungainly, verbose, and even incorrect sentence, we now have a reasonably dynamic and meaningful one.

The next sentence starts out all right, but then returns to the imprecise *one* device:

. . . if one is not fortunate enough to visit countries such as Czechoslovakia, one can still learn to appreciate what he/she has. . . .

Even the rather innocuous expression *countries such as Czechoslovakia* can be improved. The point being made does not require a plural, and the perhaps pretentious *such as* can be replaced by a simple *like*. Using *a person* to replace the entirely vague *one* and making the flow a bit more dynamic, we might come up with this:

. . . even a person who is not fortunate enough to visit a country like Czechoslovakia can still learn to appreciate what advantages he or she has. . . .

(I have also tried to make the final phrase slightly more precise by adding a noun after the vague *what*.)

The final section seems especially uneconomical:

. . . by just stopping a moment and thinking about what freedom really means and how different our way of living would be if we were deprived of it . . . if we would just put a little more thought into that one word that says so much: *Freedom.*

What is the difference between "stopping a moment and *thinking*" and "putting *a little more thought* into"?

No doubt this idea is repeated here for emphasis, but it does seem that the two "thought" processes being referred to could actually be distinguished. In the first case, we are being advised to *imagine* how different our lives would be without freedom, and in the second instance, we are being asked just to *think* about the meaning of a word.

Also, notice that we again encounter an obscure reference to "what freedom really means" *before* the idea of words and meaning has been introduced.

Finally, it also seems significant that the parallel phrasing at the end, two *if* clauses one right after the other, does not in fact reflect parallel thought or ideas. The true parallel to the last clause is first stated in a *by -ing* phrase.

Taking all of these weaknesses into account, the student writer might be able to produce the following revision:

. . . just by stopping to imagine for a moment how different our lives would be if we were deprived of them, just by putting a little more thought into that one word that says so much: *freedom.*

The parallel phrasing is emphatic, as is the return to the article's title; but in this form, the ideas are not in fact repetitive.

THE WHOLE REVISION PROCESS

Only by revising this patiently and carefully can the student writer hope to improve the degree to which his or her writing communicates correctly and effectively. *Talking about* the revision process, as I have been doing, may take much longer (and is probably harder to understand) than actually doing it.

In this case, the first review for general coherence and sense would have taken only five or ten minutes. The review for habitual errors may have taken as much as fifteen minutes, since quite a few errors had to be corrected (perhaps more than normal). The final review for incidental errors and stylistic weaknesses may have taken as much as half an hour. But at most the whole revision process, undertaken thoroughly and painstakingly, would have added an hour to the author's composition time.

It would have been an hour well spent.

Chapter XV

THE FINAL VERSION

After at most one hour of revision, the rough draft we saw in Chapter XIII would have been transformed into this finished essay:

One Word Says Much

"Most Americans take freedom for granted until they see what it's like to live without it," according to Ms. Elizabeth L. Pool, Senior High biology teacher who has just returned from a trip to Czechoslovakia. .

Ms. Pool and her husband, a tax consultant, traveled in Europe for about six weeks. Among the countries they visited were Eng-· land, France, Austria, and Germany, as well as Czechoslovakia. The Pools found this trip not only new and exciting, but also educational. "We saw so many things I never dreamt we would, and I learned so many things, it was as if a dream had come true," Ms. Pool said recently.

Ms. Pool found Czechoslovakia particularly striking. It brought to her attention several aspects of her own life she had never thought about or had merely taken for granted.

The first city the Pools visited was Prague, or as some people call it, "The City of the Thousand Towers." According to Ms. Pool, Prague is a city of diversity and beauty. Most of the castles and cathedrals have stood through eleven centuries, witnessing the many changes Prague has endured. Today, Ms. Pool notes, these majestic structures hover over modern houses, offices, apartment buildings, parks, and subway lines.

The appearance of the whole country is beautiful, but the Pools discovered that this beauty is superficial. On seeing the country's inhabitants, Ms. Pool said, the visitor immediately notices that their lives lack one essential factor. Since 1945 Czechoslovakia has

158

been an Iron Curtain country; thus the people have been deprived to some degree since then of the greatest gift a nation can offer: freedom. Today, the people have virtually no rights at all. For example, they do not have the right to own a house, to choose a career, or to travel to any country outside the Communist domain. Most important, however, they do not have freedom of speech, freedom of the press, or a truly substantial freedom of religion.

The people, according to Ms. Pool, cannot express their thoughts publicly. It is unheard of for a Czech to criticize the government, while the citizen of a free nation can always speak what he or she thinks, either praising or disapproving the country's governing body.

The Czech people, Ms. Pool learned, may practice the religion of their choice; however, they are treated as outcasts by the government for doing so. In a free nation, on the other hand, a person can be a Catholic, Protestant, Buddhist, Lutheran, or whatever she or he pleases without fearing any intervention from the government.

Finally, in Czechoslovakia, all means of communication (radio, television, newspapers, magazines) are controlled by the government, and therefore, a very limited amount of only government-selected material can be broadcast or printed. Any foreign news the government feels does not agree with its way of thinking cannot be published. This is not true in free nations; various private companies or individuals own and control the various means of communication.

These are just a few of the rights we take for granted, according to Ms. Pool, without realizing that many nations around the world have nothing at all comparable to them. In speaking with some of the people in Czechoslovakia, Ms. Pool adds, a visitor learns that before the recent Russian take-over, after which all rights were suppressed, Czechoslovakia was a peace-loving country with a stable and satisfying government. The people were content with their growing freedom and worked hard to better themselves and their country. Since the Soviets took over Czechoslovakia, the people have no desire to improve themselves or their country because they know that they would not benefit from the improvement themselves; rather, only the government would gain still more power over them.

The citizen of a free nation does not appreciate the value of freedom and of civil rights until he or she observes the lack of them elsewhere, Ms. Pool's experience would indicate. It is unfortunate indeed, she feels, that human nature works this way, but she thinks that even a person who is not lucky enough to visit a country like Czechoslovakia can still learn to appreciate what advantages he or she has, just by stopping to imagine for a moment how different our lives would be if we were deprived of them, and by putting just a little more thought into that one word that says so much: *freedom.*

When the writer of such a story as "One Word Says Much" has had more experience, she or he will not have to spend so long on the revision process. Some errors and stylistic weaknesses will disappear from the first draft; those that remain will be easier to locate and to correct. But no one learns how to write correctly and effectively without careful and painstaking revision, now and whenever possible throughout the writer's career.

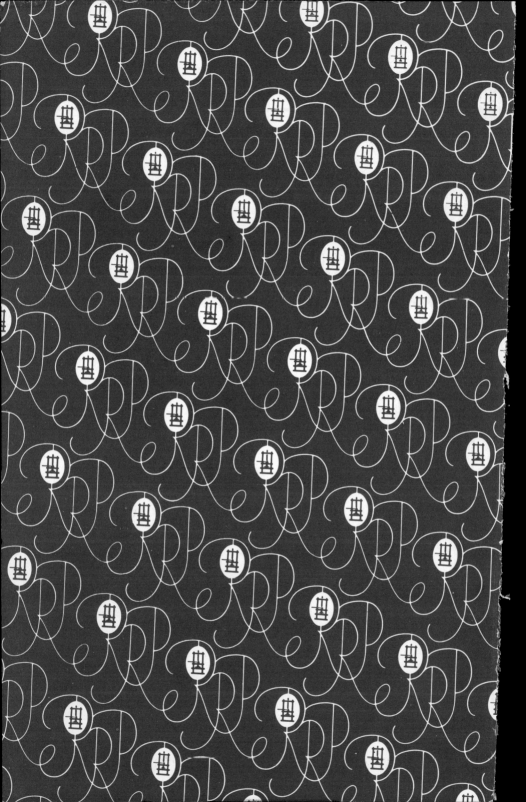

GUIDELINES
FOR BOOK CATALOGS

Book Catalogs Committee
Resources and Technical Services Division
American Library Association

American Library Association